HOPE for the MISSION

"Combining his robust theological training with over a decade of rooted experience with unhoused neighbors, Kevin Nye highlights clear-eyed, practical examples of what happens when Christians take their faith seriously enough to participate in God's reign on earth. This book ignited my imagination and solidified my resolve.

—**Shannan Martin**, author of *Counterweights*, *Start with Hello*, and *The Ministry of Ordinary Places*

"With deep wisdom and courageous truth-telling, Nye brings unique insight on key ways in which the church has failed to love God and our unhoused neighbors. This book isn't pontification from someone throwing stones from the outside; it's wisdom shaped from encountering Jesus on the margins as a seasoned practitioner."

—**Joash P. Thomas**, public theologian and author of *The Justice of Jesus*

"Nye asks hard questions and invites us to consider whether those approaches to ending homelessness are truly the best way forward. As a data nerd, I appreciate Nye's commitment to following the evidence. As an atheist, I appreciate that our values around ending homelessness are functionally identical. Nye remains one of the voices crying out in the capitalist wilderness, reminding us that we already know how to fix this, and that churches can and must lead the way."

—**Tori Williams Douglas**, antiracism educator, speaker, writer, and podcaster

"*Hope for the Mission* offers welcome alternatives to approaches that blame people for their homelessness and either punish them through criminalization or paternalistically aim to transform them. Based on his belief that we won't solve homelessness without churches, Nye emphasizes community-building and highlights the gift of knowing our unhoused neighbors and letting their experiences guide efforts to ensure that all are housed and at home."

—**Laura Stivers**, professor of ethics and co-chair of the Division of Public Affairs at Dominican University of California and author of *Disrupting Homelessness*

"*Hope for the Mission* is honest about the harm done in the name of Jesus, courageous in its critique of broken systems, and relentless in its insistence that there is a better way. This book isn't just about ending homelessness, it's about recovering the heart of the gospel: dignity, belonging, and a home for everyone."

—**Zach W. Lambert**, pastor and bestselling author of *Better Ways to Read the Bible*

"May this book be a balm and a call to action for anyone who finds themselves wondering how we can support our unhoused neighbors. Nye kindles a rare and holy hope that the end of homelessness is not just possible, but within reach."

—**Amy Kenny**, author of *My Body Is Not a Prayer Request*

"*Hope for the Mission* is a prophetic and practical call to the church to move beyond charity toward justice. With compassion, clarity, commitment, and courage, Nye shows that faith and evidence-based action are not opposites but partners in the struggle to end homelessness."

—**Liz Theoharis**, co-chair of the Poor People's Campaign and director of the Kairos Center for Religions, Rights, and Social Justice

"*Hope for the Mission* presents many ways to express Christian faith in work with and for people experiencing homelessness: hospitality, radical acceptance, advocacy, community, and joy can carry people in need much further than individual conversion. I commend this book to anyone looking to connect the dots between their own missional faith and work with people living on our streets."

—**Sara Fischer**, Episcopal priest and author of *Open: Adventures in Radical Hospitality*

"So many of our policies and practices don't actually reduce homelessness. It is hard to feel hopeful and easy to feel daunted right now; this book offers both hope and the ability to see what we can do as people of faith and people whose hearts call us to ensure that all God's children are housed."

—**Sandhya Rani Jha**, anti-oppression consultant and author of *Rebels, Despots, and Saints*

HOPE for the MISSION

Getting It Right in the Call to End Homelessness

Kevin Nye

Harrisonburg, Virginia

Herald Press
PO Box 866, Harrisonburg, Virginia 22803
www.HeraldPress.com

Library of Congress Cataloging-in-Publication Data
Names: Nye, Kevin author
Title: Hope for the mission : getting it right in the call to end homelessness / Kevin Nye.
Description: Harrisonburg, Virginia : Herald Press, [2026] | Includes bibliographical references.
Identifiers: LCCN 2025040472 (print) | LCCN 2025040473 (ebook) | ISBN 9781513816944 paperback | ISBN 9781513816951 ebook
Subjects: LCSH: Church work with the homeless | Homelessness—Religious aspects—Christianity | BISAC: RELIGION / Christian Living / Social Issues | SOCIAL SCIENCE / Social Classes & Economic Disparity
Classification: LCC BV4456 .N94 2026 (print) | LCC BV4456 (ebook)
LC record available at https://lccn.loc.gov/2025040472
LC ebook record available at https://lccn.loc.gov/2025040473

The Author is represented by and this book is published in association with the literary agency of WordServe Literary Group, Ltd., www.wordserveliterary.com.

Study guides are available for many Herald Press titles at www.HeraldPress.com.

HOPE FOR THE MISSION

Distributed by Herald Press, Harrisonburg, Virginia 22803. 800-245-7894.

Library of Congress Control Number: 2025040472
International Standard Book Number: 978-1-5138-1694-4 (paperback); 978-1-5138-1695-1 (ebook)
Printed in United States of America
Cover and interior design by Merrill Miller
Cover art by Hatsak Katsiaryna/Getty Images

30 29 28 27 26 10 9 8 7 6 5 4 3 2 1

To Naomi, Micah, and Jordan—
all of this is for you, from you, and because of you.

CONTENTS

Foreword

In my first real job in homeless services I worked closely with two Catholic nuns, Sister Rose and Sister Bernice. These two women were as different as they could be in almost every respect—their approach to the work, their roles in the organization, their interactions with me and the other young VISTA volunteers who made up a portion of the staff. But despite their differences, it was their shared deep faith, compassion, and commitment to our mission that stood out to me. Sister Rose was quite advanced in age but was still showing up every day to answer the phones and welcome women experiencing homelessness and domestic violence when they walked through our front door. Sister Bernice spent her time ministering to the women and families who came to us for help, never judging and always finding ways to offer our program participants the support they needed to realize their goals. I learned a lot from them and have carried that experience with me throughout my career in homelessness assistance.

That was more than thirty years ago, and I have since traveled many paths in my career—from a decade in federal government service and numerous positions in nonprofit spaces to my current role as CEO of the National Alliance to End Homelessness. When I started to see Kevin Nye at conferences and other shared learning spaces several years ago, I became curious about his work, especially with the publication of his first book, *Grace Can Lead Us Home*.

But I will be honest, it was a viral tweet of his that really captured my attention.

In it, Kevin described the experience of administering the emergency medication Narcan to a man overdosing on the street. I was impressed with the way he chose to use his platform—using facts, humor, and faith to draw people in. To make the point that every life is precious and valuable. That carrying Narcan is part of how he lives out his own faith.

So when he reached out with an advance copy of his second book, *Hope for the Mission*, it was easy to say yes to writing this foreword. And as expected, his values-centered approach is as thoughtful as it is effective.

Since my days working with Sister Rose and Sister Bernice, I have seen that faith-based organizations are essential to homelessness response in the United States. Many of our response systems were built on the work of faith-based groups and missions, as this book explains. In every job I have held, I have seen faith-based organizations underpin a vital part of homelessness response, and in some communities, faith-based providers are the only available form of assistance. They can hold deep influence over how the broader community responds to their homeless neighbors—whether that response treats people in need of help with compassion and dignity, or whether it judges them as less than. I have seen firsthand that when the values of these organizations align with best practices, they have positive outcomes for people experiencing homelessness. And when they don't, the harm can be significant. Kevin captures that unique dynamic in this book.

Kevin shows us through real-world examples that building bridges and working together *is the path* to ending homelessness in our nation. He shows us programs that are meeting the moment through evidence-based approaches and community-led response while also adhering to their calling as Christian organizations. *Hope for the Mission* lays out a path that leads with community and hope and joy. And it leads with evidence about what works.

We know how to end homelessness. In the United States, veteran homelessness has decreased 55 percent since 2010, in large part because secular, government, and faith-based leaders alike stood together to advocate for increased funding and programs grounded in compassionate and effective practices. If we can do it for veterans, we can do it for everyone. And faith-based partners can and should be part of the solution.

At a time of deep division in this nation, when rising rents are forcing people into the streets at rates higher than I have ever seen in my thirty-year career, those of us doing this work cannot afford to lose hope. I can't afford to lose hope. And by the time I read the final page of this book, I had tears in my eyes because I felt seen, and I think you will as well. The complexity of our feelings about the injustice of homelessness, the haunting feeling of being warm in our beds when others are outside, the rage we feel about how our society treats people deemed unworthy—these are all named not as something to feel ashamed of, but as part of what it means to live our lives with hope and faith.

Knowing that I am working alongside individuals like Kevin Nye and the people highlighted in this book brings me faith that ending homelessness is not only possible—it is inevitable.

I think that would make Sister Rose and Sister Bernice proud.

—Ann Oliva
CEO of the National Alliance to End Homelessness

Introduction

Do not let your hearts be troubled. Believe in God, believe also in me. In my Father's house there are many dwelling places. If it were not so, would I have told you that I go to prepare a place for you?

—JOHN 14:1–2

If I'm being honest, lately it's been difficult for me to follow Jesus' advice in this passage. My heart has been extremely troubled. I wonder if yours is too.

Homelessness in North America is as bad as it's ever been. On a single night in January of 2024, when the United States conducted its annual point-in-time count, we found more than six hundred fifty thousand people were experiencing homelessness, including over one hundred thousand children. Over the full course of that year, it's estimated that the number of people who experienced homelessness for at least one night exceeds one million. Those experiencing unsheltered homelessness—meaning living outside or in vehicles as opposed to shelters or interim housing—is over two hundred fifty thousand. Each of these numbers represents an all-time high.[1] Canada, which conducts its count less often, saw a 20 percent increase from 2018 to 2022.[2]

And while the numbers are indeed distressing, I can also say the promise of ending homelessness feels closer than it's ever been. Utilizing evidence-based principles such as Housing First—the practice of permanently housing people as soon as possible and then surrounding them with services—cities have made impressive strides in decreasing homelessness. Our government and nonprofit response systems are more efficient than ever when it comes to helping people find their way out of homelessness and into permanent, stable housing. Homelessness is worsening not because we don't know how to resolve it, but because the rate at which people fall into homelessness continues to accelerate. During a five-year period starting in 2019, the number of people who entered emergency shelters for the first time increased more than 23 percent. Put another way, we've become much better at bailing water, but the boat is filling even faster.

I wonder if the disciples felt this same tension between despair and hope when Jesus tried to comfort their troubled hearts. The words of the epigraph are part of a three-chapters-long oration by Jesus, which John places between Jesus' arrival in Jerusalem and his eventual arrest at the hands of the authorities. In this oration, which takes place on the evening of their Last Supper together, Jesus predicts who will betray him, prepares his disciples for what is to come next, and assures them regarding what will follow. I imagine Jesus said much of this while, one by one, he washed the feet of his disciples. When Jesus promised, "In my father's house there are many dwelling places . . . and I go there to prepare a place for you," he may have been hunched over, postured lower than a servant, using his hands to rub the dirt from their soles.

In this moment, both despair and hope fill the room: the disciples had expected that the Messiah would parade triumphantly into Jerusalem, only to learn that he was instead to be betrayed and crucified; they are at the same time promised a place in glory while submitting to a vulnerable, intimate act by God's own Son. Where desperation and holy longing comingle, a powerful movement of God is often close at hand.

Lately I've been pondering how Jesus describes his Father's house, especially because so much of my work involves housing and the concept of *home*. For the last decade, I've worked in direct services for people experiencing homelessness, and for the last half of those years—since my first book was released—I've been in dialogue and shared work with people of faith who are trying to better understand and get involved. This is one of many scriptures referring to houses or homes that I've come to read very differently since beginning this work.

Beneath the surface of this passage, but intrinsic to its meaning, is a distinction between a house and a *home*. In the English translations we're accustomed to, we read either "in my Father's house there are many rooms" (NIV) or "in my Father's house there are many dwelling-places" (NRSV). Simple one-to-one translation is tricky because the Greek words for *house* and *room/dwelling place* are loaded with meaning. The word translated *house* (*oikos*) is extremely common, always meaning *house* or *home*, but the word for *rooms* or *dwelling places* (*mone*) is extremely rare. The only other time it's used in the New Testament is just a few verses later in John 14:23, where Jesus says, "'Those who love me will keep my word, and my Father will love them, and we will come to them and make our home [*mone*] with them.'" This anticipates the coming of the Holy Spirit, which Jesus goes on to detail more fully.

If *oikos* refers to a literal house—the actual, physical place where someone lives—then *mone* is closer to what we mean when we talk about *home*. *Mone* is the intangibles that can come to fill a literal residence: love, safety, security, warmth, connection, joy. *Oikos* consists of the four walls, the roof, and the door; *mone* entails a spiritual rootedness and belonging. In this sense, I prefer a looser but more expressive translation: "In my father's house, there is room enough for everyone to belong."

This marks one more way we have fallen short of God's best for the world—where things are not "on earth as it is in heaven." Because of how we have arranged, organized, distributed, and withheld resources, there are those without *oikos* and *mone*; they have neither the literal structure of a house or apartment unit, nor the spiritual qualities that enable us to feel *home*. If housing and *homing* are both physical and spiritual, then homelessness must be too.

This book is about the ways the concrete realities of homelessness and housing are also deeply spiritual, and it's about the role that people and communities of faith could play in meeting the interconnected physical and spiritual needs of unhoused people. That said, my thesis is *not* that the North American church is the institution that will finally solve homelessness all on its own. Everyone, at an individual and institutional level, has a role to play.

What I am convinced of, more than ever, is that we won't solve homelessness *without* churches. This is a critical time for a concerted movement from within the Christian faith community to draw upon our vast physical and spiritual resources and meet the current moment. If we can all manage to row together in the same direction, homelessness really could become a thing of the past.

Right now, however, we are not a united front. The Christian witness regarding homelessness is torn between two primary camps, and most Christians are unaware of the divide, let alone how to bridge it.

On one end stands a historic institution: gospel rescue missions. Sometimes referred to as rescue missions, gospel missions, or just "missions," these ministries have dominated the Christian voice on homelessness and how to respond to it, with approximately three hundred locations operating across the United States and Canada for more than a century. While they have no centralized leadership, the vast majority are part of the CityGate Network (formerly the Association of Gospel Rescue Missions and the International Union of Gospel Missions). CityGate gathers these hundreds of independent entities under their vision and offers resources such as training, technical support, legal representation, and access to the broader network. While divergence in practices is technically allowed, CityGate has historically been clear about the core values that should animate gospel rescue missions, and there is little deviation among affiliates.

Gospel rescue missions traditionally operate from a framework that prioritizes spiritual transformation over advocacy and empowerment. They purport to provide both material and spiritual assistance to people experiencing poverty and homelessness. However, the material resources tend to be short-term: food, clothing, showers, and overnight shelter (all of which are needed, of course). But the Missions' indifference to broader, long-term solutions betrays an individualistic view of homelessness. In the eyes of rescue missions, homelessness is simply the end point of any one person's regrettable choices, rather than something imposed by systemic forces upon society's most vulnerable.

Through the lens of this flawed individualism, missions understand their long-term goal as the wholesale transformation of individuals, especially via conversion to Christianity. Providing direct services and pathways out of homelessness are merely a means of accomplishing this goal, to the extent that these services are often withheld if a person does not participate in the religious aspects of their organization. Whether rescue missions are wont to admit it, intrinsic to this understanding is the belief that homelessness is a spiritual failure—that if you turn to Jesus, then your life will begin to come together in ways that were not possible before. To this end, rescue missions have historically required religious practices—chapel attendance and Bible studies, for example—in order to receive or continue receiving services. Exploring this history, and even some of the ways it has evolved, will be crucial to understanding how we got here, and so we will spend our time there in the first couple of chapters.

At the other end of this spectrum stands a wide assortment of largely unknown, unassuming, disparate groups, all united by a commitment to truly solving homelessness in their communities and informed by their deep faithfulness. They recognize that the needs are immense and compounding, and that addressing them requires much more than a prayer or conversion. This book is predominantly for and about these people and groups. If nothing else, I hope to present a chorus of voices to rival the gospel rescue missions' prominence; an assemblage of stories in which faith compels thoughtful, evidence-based action that prioritizes human flourishing over religious affiliation.

Most books or articles that broach the topic of addressing homelessness would pause right about now to honor or affirm the good intentions behind what may ultimately be harmful practices. I'm not going to do that here, for a reason that is core to the beliefs of this book: *intention is irrelevant*. This may sound harsh, but please understand I say this in the utmost good faith. I always assume that everyone engaged in this work means well. In all my years in homelessness services, I've rarely met anyone working in this field, unglamorous and low-paying as it is, who didn't genuinely believe they were helping—or at least trying to.

When we center the intentions of those providing services, we decenter the people impacted by our work. When we enter into this work either professionally or as a volunteer, we are stepping into spaces rife with vulnerability and powerlessness. The risk of creating or contributing to harm is immensely high, and it's the responsibility of those who hold power and capacity to mitigate that. While I've rarely met anyone doing the work for the wrong reasons, I have witnessed many programs cause immense harm. The feelings and intentions behind the damage done are simply trivial in light of the stakes.

Another key pillar of this book is a commitment to Housing First principles. Housing First is an evidence-based approach that informs not only how I write about homelessness but all of the work that I do. It affirms that homelessness is a solvable problem, and that the key element to solving it begins with housing. By leading with housing, homelessness is resolved—you're no longer "homeless" if you have a home! But housing is also the foundation upon which an individual can address whatever it was that made them vulnerable to homelessness in the first place and, with wraparound support and encouragement from those with resources, they can build off this "home base" to transform their life how they see fit.

As we'll explore, the rescue mission model does not align with this approach, instead requiring people to undertake herculean efforts in the midst of their homelessness to earn the right to live independently. Life transformation—in the narrowly defined ways prescribed by the mission—is a *prerequisite* to housing. Because they hold the baseline belief that homelessness is an individual failure, and because they conflate individual failure with lack of faith, missions prioritize religious adherence over all else. When people don't succeed in these programs, they blame the individual—and no one stops to ask whether it's the program, not the individual, that is innately flawed.

In my first book, *Grace Can Lead Us Home*, I contend that the Christian notion of grace ought to be the primary lens we bring to the issue of homelessness and people who experience it. When we do this, we end up listening more than talking. We approach homelessness, and those who experience it, with curiosity rather than judgment. This book aims to take that same methodology to a program-design level: Interventions intended to address homelessness should exemplify the belief that every person has inherent worth endowed by God, and an understanding that when basic needs have been met (as articulated by them, not you), people succeed on their own terms. Rather than building programs based on our determinations, we have to, alongside those with lived experience, build ones that match the incredible needs *and* potential of the people they are designed to serve. The programs highlighted in these pages have all, to some extent, used this listening and partnering model—some from the outset, and others after much-needed reflection and reevaluation.

To this end, the examples assembled here share a steadfast belief in community and solidarity—that power is not exerted *over*, but shared *with*. While they may adopt any number of formal structures—leadership, professional standards, rules, and organization—they nonetheless strive to elevate the voices, experiences, and expertise of those they serve. They make case plans *with* people rather than *for* them, and partnership is key to any success. People aren't told to pull themselves up by their bootstraps, but they also aren't coerced into action.

The final tenet of this book, and perhaps its most crucial, is that you can focus on ending homelessness in ways that center dignity and empowerment without leaving Jesus behind. In fact, there ought to be no discrepancy between being faith-based and being evidence-based in your practice. Every program elevated in this book has grown out of a deep commitment to the ways of Jesus, and each one continues to embody that commitment—even as some have incorporated as faith-based nonprofits and others have grown in different directions.

Parsing how this works itself out means developing a mature understanding of spirituality. In believing that homelessness is the result of moral and spiritual deficiencies, rescue missions have prioritized conversion and spiritual transformation over meeting the long-term material needs of the people who enter their doors. Because of this, they may boast large numbers of "new believers" but very little success in ending homelessness.

But rescue missions misunderstand even the spiritual needs of those who venture inside their walls. In focusing on a profession of faith and conversion experience, they miss the deep enmeshment of spiritual needs with physical ones. When it comes to homelessness, a lack of material resources is usually intertwined with a lack of community, acceptance, and care for the inner life of a person. To experience homelessness implies not just a lack of a house, but the lack of a *home*: the physical space imbued with a sense of stability, comfort, and rest. Homelessness is a crisis with both physical and spiritual repercussions.

Because of this, the church is uniquely positioned to address this dual crisis of house and home. The faith that energizes us, and the institutions that undergird us, empower us to engage homelessness in ways that the government either cannot or does not. But if we imagine the spirituality of homelessness in terms of dogma or creed, we will always fall short of meeting people's true needs. The groups highlighted in this book all understand this, and they act on it in myriad ways.

A common question I hear in my work is, "What should our church do?" And I struggle to respond because the options are seemingly endless. In this book you will find many such pathways in the form of churches and faithful groups who are in their own unique ways and in their own unique contexts responding to this same question. To conclude each of the chapters with such stories, you will find a section called "Go and Do Likewise." These sections highlight the tangible takeaways from those doing similar work. While there is no pre-written playbook for engaging homelessness in your context, there are examples of those who have gone before. Perhaps one of them will resonate so much that it illuminates your path clearly and specifically. More likely, and more in line with my hopes in sharing these, is that each of them nestles itself within you in its own way. By internalizing these stories and the hopes and heartaches that inspired them, you may find their imagination contagious and chart a way forward as unique to you and your community as they are to theirs.

You will also encounter a sort of trajectory in the structure of this book. After examining the history and practices of gospel rescue missions, with an eye toward understanding how this work hasn't always been done well, we'll begin looking at churches and organizations who are living out a different way. They are grouped into categories, some of which fit more precisely than others. Many of the groups highlighted could have been placed in any number of the categories and had to be arranged with some eye to practicality. But the placement of the chapters is intentionally designed to demonstrate a movement from responsiveness in the form of mercy, to solidarity that pursues justice. You will meet churches who used their land to create housing, and then others who took that work further into challenging the injustices of housing policy beyond their property lines. You will see churches who began small ministries offering basic needs, who then allowed the relationships they developed to lead them into work that cultivated dignity, joy, and liberative action. In the latter chapters, you will meet organizations who carefully maintain Christian spiritual practices among their homelessness ministry, without making them mandated, coercive, or abusive—including a rescue mission!

The selection of the programs and organizations in this book is imperfect and non-exhaustive. Because it's filtered through my experiences and exposure, it will by necessity overlook countless amazing stories and examples. The exclusion of a particular group certainly does not mean I don't support their work—I may have simply not encountered them yet, or perhaps I couldn't fit them in. Additionally, the inclusion of an organization or program doesn't necessarily mean I support and agree with every aspect of their work. Organizations, like individuals, are complicated and messy—they change over time as leaders come and go, and they don't always live up to their reputation. I have done my best to seek confirmation of the work being done by witnessing it firsthand or speaking to diverse sources involved: those working on the frontlines at these organizations, community partners, and even those receiving services.

I also want to note that there is no amount of research, work, or accompaniment that I—someone who has been stably and comfortably housed my entire life—could do to become more an "expert" on homelessness compared to those who have lived it themselves. This book, and all my work, aims to embolden, bolster, and amplify the voices that are so often shunned, and who rarely get an audience due to the ways we've organized our society. In doing so, however, another risk emerges: When individuals and organizations seek to include and uplift stories of marginalization, people who have experienced trauma face the dilemma of reliving it for the benefit of others and little for themselves. To write about homelessness in the midst of these realities with integrity demanded I did the following, at minimum: All individuals I interviewed who had lived experience of homelessness were compensated for both their expertise and their emotional labor. Additionally, two individuals—one currently unhoused and one formerly—were paid to read the text and give feedback on its content, tone, and language, resulting in additions, changes, and clarity. While not comprehensive, and still an imperfect substitute, I hope that this book better represents the truth of homelessness academically, theologically, and experientially.

How we work together to end homelessness is the utmost consideration of this book. In this way, this is ultimately a book about hope. This hope is not based on disconnected, pie-in-the-sky feelings, but rooted in a deep sense of the way things could be and ought to be. Cole Arthur Riley has written extensively on the deep connection of lament and hope, concluding that "lament is not anti-hope. It's not even a stepping-stone to hope. Lament itself is a form of hope. It's an innate awareness that what is should not be. As if something is written on our hearts that tells us exactly what we are meant for, and whenever confronted with something contrary to this, we experience a crumbling."[3]

For this reason, the traditional model of the gospel rescue mission, in its myriad iterations, will be open for scrutiny. Addressing harm is an act of hope in that it refuses to resign to the way things are when a better world is possible. But rather than a book about what's going wrong, this is a celebration of what's going right. While the first couple chapters will intimately interrogate rescue missions and their legacy, the vast majority of the book will highlight programs and organizations across the country who have synchronized their hearts to the beat of God's when it comes to homelessness and created programs and movements that bear good fruit.

* * *

> My heart is beating out of my chest right now thinking that I may get a chance to really tell my story. I'll need to sleep on it and get back to you—I carry trauma from my homeless experiences, especially my experiences at the mission.

Sarah (a pseudonym) wrote this to me our first time chatting. I had posted a statistic on social media that got shared a few times. It was based on a study indicating that a hundred-dollar increase in median rent was associated with a 9 percent increase in homelessness. Sarah messaged me, asking for my source—not as an accusation, but so she could use it in her own advocacy work. I shared the source, and we chatted a bit about homelessness, advocacy, and the Supreme Court. She shared with me that she had lived for two years at the Grants Pass Gospel Rescue Mission in Oregon.

At the time, the Supreme Court was deliberating a case called *Johnson v Grants Pass*. The crux of this case was whether or not the US Constitution allowed cities to criminalize homelessness—and if so, under what circumstances. The city of Grants Pass, Oregon, had defied a lower court's ruling and resumed a policy of aggressive criminalization against the city's unhoused population. The Supreme Court ended up ruling in favor of the city and overturning the previous court decision that had put some limitations on criminalization. As of their decision in the summer of 2024, it is considered legal at the federal level to criminalize homelessness regardless of the number or accessibility of resources.

This hit hard for Sarah, as she knew firsthand that in the city of Grants Pass (and many cities throughout North America), the only services available are those of the local gospel rescue mission. When I finally got to hear Sarah's story (which you'll read more about in chapter 2), I was confronted with the breadth of harm that these institutions can inflict in the name of Jesus, and the long-lasting impact it can have on individuals and communities.

Sarah's story isn't ultimately about her degradation or humiliation—at least, that's not where it ends. Sarah's story is about resilience, recovery, and *hope*. She takes seriously the harm that was done to her during that phase of life, including but not limited to the Grants Pass Mission, while also downright refusing to let that define who she is or will be.

This book borrows from her hope too.

In a sense, this book is only about rescue missions insofar as Sarah's story is. The first two chapters are going to tell serious stories, unearth complex history, and tell the hard-to-swallow truth about what missions are, have done, and are doing. As we move through these chapters, "hope for the mission" may mean a number of different things. I offer that it can function as an invitation to gospel rescue missions to see themselves in light of those who have been harmed by their practices and in contrast to alternative ways of faithfully answering the call to end homelessness.

It may also mean that hope lies in the true *mission*—ending homelessness—regardless of the destiny of gospel rescue missions. I do not say that lightly, as more than anything, this book is about hope—identifying Christian faithfulness in the face of the growing crisis of homelessness. In these pages, you will find far more ideas of what to do than what *not* to do—far more examples to emulate than foes to criticize. The future of gospel rescue missions remains uncertain, but the *mission* of ending homelessness—and doing so for the sake of Christ—is renewed daily by those who take Christ at his word that the least of these are first in God's ordering of the universe. Christians all over the world are embracing *this* mission, and we have an opportunity to join them.

This book is for all those whose hearts beat for a better world. For those like me whose hearts have been deeply troubled not simply because of how bad things are, but because they hope and believe that they can be better. For those like Sarah, whose hearts beat outside of their chests with the opportunity to be seen and heard as someone worthy of housing and worthy of *home*; to know that their stories are worth telling and worth hearing and believing enough to change how we do things.

Even as homelessness has worsened in the last few years, I have not lost hope. Even as the Supreme Court has made ending homelessness even harder by allowing for criminalization without requiring resources of any kind, let alone quality, I remain hopeful—because I believe God is at work, always doing a new thing among us. I am hopeful because Sarah is hopeful. For her to have the courage not only to tell her story but to take up the cause of ending homelessness is the ultimate act of hope. Like the thousands of people I've met over the years who are experiencing or have experienced homelessness, she believes life can be better not just for her, but for all of us.

Leaning on their strength, I can believe that too—and I remain convinced that Christians have a decisive role to play in making that possible. This book is for everyone whose heart beats out of their chest when they encounter homelessness, who anticipates the world God imagines for us and all the ways we are short of it, and who humbly and confessionally offers themselves and their communities into that difference. My prayer is that you are convicted, inspired, affirmed, and energized by the work witnessed in this book, and that God does a new thing in you—and then through you.

ONE

Jerry McAuley's Dream Diluted

When Jerry McAuley was released from prison in 1864, he longed for a place that would feed both his body and his spirit. In prison he had found Jesus, but outside he found a world even more hostile to him than when he had gone in. "If any one had spoken to me kindly and in a Christian spirit at that time, it would have subdued me," he wrote in his autobiography. "But no one came near the poor, wretched outcast."[1]

He was no stranger to scorn. When McAuley was an infant in Ireland, his father fled authorities who had grown wise to his counterfeiting schemes. His mother sent him to live with his grandmother, who then sent him to America to live with his sister. Before long, he was slumming on Water Street—part of the skid row area of East Manhattan, New York—committing crimes of survival until he was framed for highway robbery and sentenced to fifteen years in Sing Sing maximum security prison.

Released and pardoned after seven years, this newly transformed man reentered a world that had changed for the worse. Mid-1800s America was a miserable place to be poor. The end of the Civil War and the boom of the railway industry made for a ballooning population of poor folks who could get around more freely than they ever had before. Communities became more porous as transient people came and went, and municipalities responded to their new unwanted neighbors in one of two ways: jail, or the poorhouse. Authorities had ultimate discretion over who went where, though the two options weren't altogether different destinations. Contemporaries described the poorhouses as "living tombs" and "social cemeteries." With limited funding, they "quickly degenerated from therapeutic to custodial establishments."[2] At the time he left prison, born-again McAuley was treated as a criminal even before he returned to his old ways.

Clawing his way out from hopelessness and alcoholism, he forced friendship on a reluctant missionary. The missionary must have seen something in Jerry beyond his initial dismissal, as he became a source of spiritual enrichment and kindness on what was to be a journey toward profound healing. After some fits and starts, Jerry secured honest work and started saving money for a vision he had: a refuge for lost souls to find physical and spiritual nourishment. His missionary friend introduced him to a wealthy benefactor who went on to donate the building that became the McAuley Water Street Mission—widely considered the first gospel rescue mission in America.

Jerry wasn't building a movement, at least not on purpose. He was building the refuge he had needed his whole life, both before and after prison. He opened it on Water Street in 1872, the same block on which he'd slummed since he was thirteen. The mission allowed poor folks to gather, eat soup and bread, and rest. In the evenings, McAuley held a prayer service that began not in condemnation, but in testimony. Sounding like the apostle Paul, "chief of sinners," Jerry began every service with his story before inviting folks to share their own.

> He saves me to-night from being a drunkard, and a gambler, and a thief, and a fraud, and everything else that you can put in. He saved me eleven years ago; and he saves me more tonight than he did then, because I've grown in grace.[3]

Something about Jerry's mission captivated and catalyzed people beyond his wildest dreams. He wanted everyone experiencing the pain he had held to also revel in the salvation he now enjoyed. The spiritual and practical were as inextricable in his work as they were in his life. As a man of faith who had experienced both the pangs of an empty stomach and the despair of a broken heart, he could deftly and inoffensively balance the work of offering bread to the hungry while sharing his experience of Jesus. He knew intimately both the goodness of God and the scorn of the church. He ran the Water Street Mission for a brief twelve years, before opening another, smaller one for women near Wall Street. Two years later, he died of tuberculosis, which he had contracted in prison and never kicked.

In a world accustomed to viewing the poor as wretched criminals, it likely felt revolutionary to treat them instead as merely lost. This is not to say there were no contemporary voices advocating for a more systemic view of poverty and homelessness. But McAuley, genuinely believing that his soul and body were both saved simultaneously by Christ, offered this opportunity to an oppressed lot of whom he'd once been a downtrodden member.

While McAuley only opened these two small missions in his brief career, it was his successors, protégés of his Water Street ministry, who dreamed of missions across the country. Perhaps inspired by the expansionist model of the Salvation Army, newly arrived from across the Atlantic, gospel missions rapidly spread from coast to coast. Something had started that even 150 years later holds a position of authority and power in the Christian landscape of poverty and homelessness.

No definitive, comprehensive history of rescue missions as they developed outward from Water Street appears to exist; nor do I intend to write one. What follows is a series of snapshots from various viewpoints over the last century and a half, orienting the rescue mission movement within the American sociopolitical and religious landscape. This narrative, in broad strokes, will elucidate how Jerry McAuley's dream became a worldwide network of hundreds of organizations, with many of their standard practices echoing McAuley's original intent and others he would hardly recognize.

* * *

The changing American landscape of poverty—fueled by the fallout of the Civil War and the ability of poor individuals to be transient in search of new opportunities—invited philosophical and theological change as well. As Jerry was starting his rescue mission, pastors and philosophers were preaching new messages about wealth and poverty that would define the world into which the rescue mission movement was born. The narratives that proliferated at that time cast a long shadow under which we still find ourselves today.

Russell Conwell, founder of Temple University and half the namesake of Gordon-Conwell Theological Seminary, was an American minister who began his ministry in 1880. While he wrote and preached countless sermons, there was one sermon he preached over six thousand times: "Acres of Diamonds." In the speech, which he delivered at churches, revivals, and universities across the country, Conwell suggests that a chief Christian responsibility was to get rich in order to wield power and further the mission of the church.

> Money is power, and you ought to be reasonably ambitious to have it! . . . Money printed your Bible, money builds your churches, money sends your missionaries, and money pays your preachers, and you would not have many of them, either, if you did not pay them.[4]

The roots of the modern-day prosperity gospel can be traced back to this sermon. Twentieth-century preachers such as Oral Roberts and Jim Bakker, along with contemporaries like pastor Joel Osteen and Christian financial advisor Dave Ramsey, have all traded in this formulation: wealth is a sign of God's blessing upon the Christian and the church (and by extension, its pastors). What is left unsaid, or more subtly implied, is that the opposite is also true: poverty is a sign of God's judgment. Conwell, for his part, felt no compunction about stating it plainly:

> I sympathize with the poor, but the number of poor who are to be sympathized with is very small. To sympathize

> with a man whom God has punished for his sins, thus to help him when God would still continue a just punishment, is to do wrong, no doubt about it, and we do that more than we help those who are deserving. While we should sympathize with God's poor—that is, those who cannot help themselves—let us remember there is not a poor person in the United States who was not made poor by his own shortcomings, or by the shortcomings of someone else. It is all wrong to be poor, anyhow.[5]

In the same period, Andrew Carnegie, at the time the wealthiest man in the world, wrote an essay entitled "Wealth," which was later circulated as "The Gospel of Wealth." Considered the foundational document for American philanthropy, the incredibly popular piece didn't just encourage generosity; it argued that the solution to the growing wealth inequality was for the wealthiest to carefully and shrewdly give of their surplus. Carnegie's conclusions dovetailed well with Conwell's: If wealth was God's blessing and poverty God's curse, then the distribution of resources to the poor should be determined by the rich. Echoing Conwell, Carnegie insisted that the wealthy should avoid giving money to organizations that help "the slothful, the drunken, the unworthy."[6]

We don't know whether the words of Conwell or Carnegie ever found their way to Jerry McAuley, but it's doubtful they would have resonated with him. While he never articulated a systemic view of poverty, McAuley knew that those with wealth and privilege were unable to see the Jesus of Water Street: "It is difficult for Christians whose position and circumstances in life when converted were those of respectability and comfort to realize all that religion—salvation through the Lord Jesus Christ—means to many of these people whose testimonies are to be heard [at the mission]."[7] McAuley went on to write that salvation for those at the mission was spiritual and tangible; transcendent and tactile. Wealth did not give a Christian special insight into the plight of the poor; in fact, quite the opposite. It was McAuley's own lifetime of experience that afforded him the right to speak to the wanderers of Water Street as one of their own.

As McAuley's missions expanded after his passing, though, it's not hard to see how that mission became diluted through these popular teachings. Where McAuley believed the poor deserved Jesus' healing as much as anyone, Conwell's theology claimed the poor were the subjects of divine judgment. Where McAuley believed proximity to the poor afforded the church an opportunity to live like Jesus, Carnegie's vision of shrewd charity taught that the wealthy ought to govern over and assess the worthiness of the poor. And as the century turned and missions propagated, lines of distinction began to form and solidify the future of the movement.

* * *

At first glance, Mary McDowell and Iva Vennard should have been allies, maybe even friends. Both grew up Methodist in late-1800s Chicago and were drawn to the plight of the poor—especially poor women—as an extension of their faith. They were both critical of an emerging governmental response to poverty they considered callous and cruel. But McDowell and Vennard instead found themselves in deep conflict over the role of religion in their ministries.

McDowell and Vennard were of a kind regarding their distaste for Charity Organization Societies (COS). Brought to New York by an English-American reverend, the role of the COS was to proliferate "scientific charity"—which on the surface aimed to simply avoid duplication and redundancy by mapping out all of the services available to the poor in a given city. In practice, they applied a Social Darwinist approach to poverty, distinguishing between those poor who were deserving and those who should be left to their own devices. Some of its biggest proponents were Christian ministers who feared that socialism was infecting the underclass, convincing them that their plight was systemic and not personal. The Christian origins of COS drew lyrical criticism from John Boyle O'Reilly, whose poem "In Bohemia" contained the eviscerating verse, "The organized charity, scrimped and iced / In the name of a cautious, statistical Christ."[8]

Despite their faith-based foundation and propagation, COS were secular in practice. Even as they intended to organize and strategize with the emerging rescue missions, leaders in the COS movement didn't care for them; not necessarily because they were too religious, but because they were too *generous*. Rescue missions like those in McAuley's mold or the Salvation Army, they believed, not only created dependence but in fact *caused* poverty. One leader went so far as to say, "A man had no right to be homeless."[9] This drew opposition from every side, from those like Iva Vennard who believed relief must also be explicitly evangelistic, to those like McDowell who believed that their obsession with categorizing individuals was fundamentally cruel.

McDowell was an early member of the settlement house movement in America. Founded by Jane Addams, settlement houses were homes designated for those facing poverty, situated alongside the homes of those more fortunate who were committed to solidarity. These houses attracted not only their technical residents, but also regular guests for meals and friendship. Mary McDowell fell in love with the model while working at the Hull House, Addams' first settlement home. She went on to start one of her own at the University of Chicago.

While faith was a central motivator in the movement's establishment, neither evangelism nor worship were essential components of its practice. Addams and her followers were students of the Social Gospel tradition, which believed that the call of Jesus was not merely to save souls but to improve social conditions. In contrast to the theology of Conwell and Carnegie, the Social Gospel aligned itself alongside the poor rather than against or over them. This faith compelled McDowell and Addams to create places of hospitality and relief based on "the impulse to share the lives of the poor, the desire to make social service, irrespective of propaganda, express the spirit of Christ."[10]

Iva Vennard, on the other hand, believed deeply in the importance of saving souls—so much that she founded multiple training schools for evangelists. Believing that Christ cared for and healed both body and spirit, she was intrigued by the emerging settlements. She was unconvinced, though, by Addams' and McDowell's resistance to proselytizing. When she was asked why she felt the need to start another settlement in Chicago, she responded, "Because we believe that foreigners, poor people, and all classes need salvation. We must do more than serve our people through humanitarian service. These temporal benefits we gladly give, but they are the bait for our hook, and we do not feel that we have ever done our best for a family until we have brought them to know Jesus."[11]

This bait and hook analogy was a metaphor that Vennard would return to frequently, and it represented a development in the mindset of the rescue mission. Jerry McAuley undoubtedly recognized that providing tangible needs provided him an audience to share his story and bring souls to Christ, but he never described it in such shrewd terms. His first successor Samuel Hadley, in part responsible for the rapid expansion of rescue missions, would say, "We generally hit a man in the stomach with a beefsteak or a loaf of bread, or both, before we pray for him."[12] This phrasing describes more of a sequence of events—which missions would soon reverse—even if it intimates a causal connection between the bread and prayer. The "bait and hook" metaphor, while likely not originating with Vennard, first appears in historical records connected to gospel rescue missions, and it would become a central facet of their reputation thereafter.

McDowell took direct issue with this. In 1908 at the National Conference of Methodist Social Workers, she declared, "Someone has said that where the mission sees sinners, the settlement sees citizens, and that where one believes in converting the individual, the other says the environment also must be converted, believing that pasture is at least as strong, if not stronger, than breed."[13]

In this same period, Joe Hill wrote his scathing parody song "The Preacher and the Slave," imitating the hymn "Sweet By and By" frequently sung at the Salvation Army (which the song refers to as the "Starvation Army"). The song's first verse and chorus describe the experience of those at the mercy of efforts that prioritize evangelism over physical needs:

Long-haired preachers come out every night,
Try to tell you what's wrong and what's right;
But when asked how 'bout something to eat
They will answer with voices so sweet:
You will eat, bye and bye,
In that glorious land above the sky;
Work and pray, live on hay,
You'll get pie in the sky when you die.[14]

Despite this opposition, rescue missions and the Salvation Army continued to grow. And when the catastrophe of the Great Depression struck, the landscape of poverty and homelessness was hit so drastically—now impacting entire families rather than primarily single adults—that disagreements on relief methods were largely suspended. Rescue missions were a large part of the backbone of relief, as the country was still a decade away from establishing federal direct aid in the form of welfare. Missions expanded their work and altered their programming to meet this morphing and exploding demand.

While they remained unquestioned by those in power, these institutions still drew the ire of the poor—though their words were, and still are, rarely documented. One of the rare works to reflect their experience was *Sister of the Road*, by Ben Reitman, who had a dedicated medical practice for the poor. He wrote the book in the style of an autobiography of one "Box-car Bertha," in actuality an amalgamation of three homeless women he had known through his practice. In Bertha's eyes we get a glimpse of Depression-era homelessness and a critique of the missions' increasing prioritization of salvation over basic needs, as well as how this prioritization was navigated:

> In the earlier days the missions and the private charities would help transients, especially women. Some of the girls made a specialty of all the words and attitudes that went with "being saved," and used them all successfully to get the watery soup and the coffee and bread that were put out by rescue missions in the name of the Lord.[15]

As Mary McDowell and Iva Vennard illustrate, the beginning of the twentieth century offered distinct visions for communities of faith to engage poverty and homelessness, drawn along ideological lines. Gospel rescue missions became increasingly associated with the "soup, soap, salvation" model of the Salvation Army, willing even to withhold the first two for the sake of the third. The Great Depression created a level of need such that communities were not apt to be discriminating, and rescue missions were poised to grow—to the adoration of the general public and to the frustration of those who would need their services, with little in the way of alternatives or power to do anything to change it. While it *ought* not be true, the aphorism is accurate when options are few: beggars can't be choosers.

* * *

Phineas Bresee, the founder of the Church of the Nazarene, the denomination in which I was born and raised, planted his first church after leaving a rescue mission. The Peniel Mission, founded by T. P. and Manie Ferguson in 1886 in downtown Skid Row, Los Angeles, was especially focused on evangelism—if they offered food or anything in the way of physical resources, you wouldn't know it from the founders' description:

> We had a noon prayer meeting every day, which still continues today to the glory of God. Street meeting every evening followed by testimonies and preaching in the hall. On Sabbath, part of the time, [T. P.] had a Bible class at 10 A.M. and preached at eleven. Street meeting at 2:30 P.M. just before the holiness meeting at 3 o'clock. At six P.M. another Bible class, then prayer and street meeting and service in the hall. A big, full, beautiful day.[16]

When Bresee joined the mission's leadership, he had other ideas in mind. He saw evangelism and conversions—objecting to neither—but what he didn't see was *church*. He wanted education, membership, community, and spiritual maturity. He and another leader broke away from the mission and began planting churches instead, named after Jesus' birthright as a "Nazarene"—an outcast, commoner, and exile.

The churches he founded merged with other holiness movements in 1908, and today the global denomination has more than thirty thousand congregations. All of this originated in Bresee's desire to offer Skid Row's poor something more spiritually rich than a "turn or burn" sermon. He wrote in his journal, "It has been my long cherished desire to have a place in the heart of the city, which could be made a center of Holy Fire, and where the gospel could be preached to the poor."[17] Bresee got his wish, founding Los Angeles First Church of the Nazarene in the heart of Skid Row.

A decade earlier, and on the opposite coast, I wonder whether Jerry McAuley might have loved Phineas Bresee's church. While Jerry was trying to find honest work and grow in his faith, he struggled to find a church that would even let him worship inside until a Methodist church finally allowed him to join—on probation. Bresee's Churches of the Nazarene welcomed the poor of downtown Los Angeles, San Francisco, and other West Coast urban centers into full church fellowship; members, not just converts.

That is, until after World War II, when Los Angeles First Church uprooted, eventually settling three miles northwest in the Koreatown neighborhood in 1953, where it continues to reside. Not even Phineas Bresee's dream could withstand the phenomenon of white flight.

White flight refers to predominantly white families leaving particular neighborhoods and communities due to increasing presence and inclusion of people of color. The most pronounced period of this phenomenon took place after World War II, when inner cities were desegregated, particularly via school assignments. Preferring exclusion, whites fled to the suburbs, established private schools, and ensured—through zoning laws, deed restrictions, and redlining—that they would not be followed.

What did follow them, though, were their churches. Like Los Angeles First Church, thousands of churches moved from downtown areas into the suburbs—sometimes moving so far that they no longer resided in the city after which they are named.

From this increased geographic distance, the church's relationship changed not only to the poor of the country's urban downtowns, but to the rescue missions as well. No longer in their own backyard, the work of rescue missions was akin to missionary work done overseas; outsourcing their call to love and serve the poor to the only faith groups willing to be near them. Rescue missions were poised to fill this vacuum, complete with their particular view of the moral and spiritual character of the residents.

Phineas Bresee planted his Nazarene congregations in inner cities because he believed the poor deserved more from a church than a rescue mission. A half century later, when all the churches moved out, the missions proved him right. Having solidified their reputation as evangelistic above all else, they operated in arms-length partnership with churches to serve as missionaries to the poor, failing to provide what Bresee—and McAuley—had imagined: kinship and shared life as siblings in Christ.

* * *

Since as early as 1906, most gospel rescue missions have been interconnected. While each entity retains its own independence in governance, hundreds are members of an organization whose purpose is to connect, empower, and proliferate the work of gospel rescue missions. This accord included the Salvation Army until its growth necessitated an amicable separation from the rescue missions. In 1913, the International Union of Gospel Missions (IUGM) incorporated, and the movement grew exponentially over the course of the next fifty-plus years.

Over that time, some of its leaders produced literature related to the work of missions, most of which is now lost. But in the 1970s, the IUGM commissioned William Sleath, a faithful steward of mission work for more than forty years, to produce a book, *Unto the Least of These*, an assembly of descriptive and prescriptive guidance from a collection of authors on what gospel rescue missions are and ought to be. With chapters on rescue mission history, recommended organizational structure, and program guidelines, this work provides the single best insight into missions' self-understanding and the synchronization of their belief system. It solidifies above all else gospel rescue missions' commitment to evangelizing the poor and unhoused, whose problems it identifies as the result of a lesser moral and spiritual constitution.

Using pejoratives like "human derelicts," the many authors of the book consistently paint the visitors of the rescue mission as helpless, selfish, inept, and, above all else, sinful. Describing the downtown skid row areas most missions inhabit, Sleath writes, "Into such areas of lost hopes and vanished dreams come these social outcasts with a desire to forget and be forgotten."[18] With this broad brush, he claims there is "one characteristic which stands out among the denizens of Skid Row—they are not concerned about the other fellow."[19] When churches come to lead worship, the book advises them, "Do not get familiar with those attending the service."[20]

In a moment of rare but poignant contrast, the author of the final chapter, "Ministering to the Whole Person," warns of the dangers of rescue mission work that stems from the elevation of the worker's ego: the chief among these being *paternalism*. The attitude of paternalism is characterized as, "I am being good to you by giving you what you need. I will do your thinking for you, and you must submit to me. You are not adequate without me for you are my product."[21] But a mere ten pages later, the same writer tells of how his parents had to force him to go to school and get educated, and concludes,

> As a result, I believe in the principle of coercion. . . . When the man or woman comes to us and says, "I want help," he

> is placing himself in our hands. . . . To allow him to make decisions is to be untrue to our obligation. If doing what he had wanted to do had been sufficient, he would never have gotten into this tragic condition.[22]

Incredibly, the same contributor warning against paternalism restates and reaffirms it in textbook fashion, using a metaphor of parenting to explain why the rescue mission must control and manipulate its guests, along with yet another reminder that their situation is of their own making. Sleath plays this point up in dramatic fashion: "The basic problem of the clients of the Mission is SIN! Regardless of how one may try to disguise it, the cause is the same. The only cure for sin is The Blood of Christ."[23]

To that end, "Every member of the Mission staff should be a Personal Evangelist."[24] While the recommendations for staff, executives, and board members include professional qualifications, they all come secondary to the insistence that they be born again, and ready to testify. Whatever assistance may or may not be offered by the rescue mission, "The goal of the IUGM is that every Rescue Mission has a Gospel Service every night."[25]

This insistence is especially interesting for the time in which the book was produced, when the makeup of the mission seeker was changing. In the 1960s, the US government closed down federal asylums for those with severe mental illness, promising instead to support community mental health clinics—a promise that never truly materialized. While this is often overemphasized as the main driver of modern homelessness (which is much more directly correlated to the slashing of Housing and Urban Development [HUD] and welfare benefits in the 1980s), it would have certainly been the experience of rescue missions to see a major influx of folks with severe mental illness showing up at their door with nowhere else to go.

For the rescue mission facing deinstitutionalization, mental health was less an opportunity to serve changing needs in a new way than it was yet another tool to maneuver the mind toward accepting Christ, as Sleath points out:

> In the nineteen seventies Rescue Missioners face a different type of person . . . to be sure the basic problem is still the same—sin—but the needs are far more complex. . . . The Rescue Mission Worker must have a practical knowledge of the techniques of counseling, psychology and psychiatry if he is to do the work of Christ in a way that will get through to the hearts of people.[26]

Rescue missions' stubbornness in prioritizing gospel proclamation above all else despite homelessness changing in size and scope began to draw academic criticism in the 1970s. A 1976 study by James Rooney focused on the content of their services as well as on the thoughts of guests and staff. In his research, Rooney attended more than two hundred services at missions across seventeen different cities and spoke with hundreds of attendees and staff.

One of the most telling findings comes from Rooney's documentation of the developed slang of the attendees. Sermons were known as *earbeatings*; *singing for your supper* referred to the requirement to worship before being fed, which included expectations to sing loudly and proudly or else delay the service; conversions were called *nosedives*, invoking the way a boxer would "take a dive" by falling to the mat in a rigged game that they were expected to lose; a *cold weather Christian* referred to the practice of feigning conversion each autumn in order to have a warm bed at a mission each winter.[27] These pejoratives highlight the recognition by those attending the services that even though the mission placed them in an uneven power dynamic against their will, they could still assert their agency in small ways.

Rooney observed that the content of the sermons and even the songs was overwhelmingly punitive, and the effect it had was one of intentional humiliation.

> One central theme dominates both: sin and the need for salvation. . . . Because the gospel service is designed to motivate an individual to accept the status of sinner, in contrast to personal rebuffs, it is a structured and systematic attack on the self-conception. The gospel service thereby serves as a devestment [*sic*] ceremony through which members of the congregation are shorn of membership in the self-supporting working class and are newly defined as belonging to a lower stratum of thoroughly inadequate persons.[28]

While the content of the sermons consistently communicated that the poverty and status of the attendees was of their own doing, mission leaders interviewed by Rooney did express some recognition of systemic forces, such as unemployment and disability—though they ranked them lower than alcoholism and lack of ambition. Rooney noted, however, that, "When mission personnel mount the pulpit, they invariably assume the institutional stance that all poverty is due to moral deficit."[29]

In 1987, a study from Ronald Fagan that surveyed thirty-seven missions in Los Angeles and Seattle backed up Rooney's findings: Fagan identified an emphasis on the worship service above all else, an obvious intent to use the need for food and shelter as "bait," and a harsh distinction between those in charge and those not. He noted that after a service, the leaders did not socialize with attendees in 60 percent of the services his study observed. Fagan also interviewed a mission director, who confirmed the overall observation of mission priorities in shocking fashion: "I feel no responsibility to feed these guys. If we drop the services, we will quit."[30]

Just over a decade later, when popular writer Ace Backwords recalled his time on the streets, he echoed these sentiments. Comparing them to the Catholic institutions which served food with "a minimum of proselytizing," he admonished:

> The Gospel Soup Kitchens, on the other hand, are generally loathed. They usually force a captive audience of hungry bums to sit through an hour-long sermon/harangue, screaming at us for being a bunch of sinners, assholes, drunks, and sodomites, before they give us our soup.[31]

Whether from the IUGM themselves or the few first-hand accounts we have, gospel rescue missions became known across the country for a recognizable set of values and practices. The existence of the IUGM (which would later become the Association of Gospel Rescue Missions in 2002, and CityGate Ministries in 2018) promoted this shared identity through literature, gatherings, and other sharing of resources. This is reminiscent of Southern Baptist churches, more than forty thousand of which are independent entities joined in association with the Southern Baptist Convention. And still, though both a twentieth-century gospel rescue mission and a Southern Baptist church lack an authoritative governing body, because of shared history, values, and practices, you could walk into any one of these across the country and know, with little variation, what to expect.

As we turn to twenty-first-century missions, we will largely move away from primary documents and engage instead with the testimonials of those who worked at or received services from missions. Like Jerry McAuley, whose own experience of being down and out on Water Street enabled him to serve as both preacher and peer, those who have seen and felt the work of the mission firsthand are our best witnesses. They bear sharper resemblance to Jerry himself than most mission leaders, and are—for better and for worse—the true inheritors of his complicated legacy.

TWO

The Behaviors and Beliefs of Gospel Rescue Missions

Sarah did not want to live at Grants Pass Gospel Rescue Mission. Reputation preceded the county's only shelter, but options had run out. It was a snowball effect: Leaving an unhealthy relationship and a prolonged recovery from surgery cost her job, then her housing. An active addiction to her pain medication followed, and suddenly Sarah had to choose between the notorious shelter and the streets.

She knew she needed help and that parts of her life needed to change, but she was afraid of what the Mission might strip her of. "My initial feeling was a deep fear," she remembers. "Fear of losing most of my rights to be the person I currently was, even if I was quite unhealthy . . . I felt like I would be losing my identity." Her fears proved legitimate. Even while undergoing a painful—and medically unsupervised—cold-turkey detox, she was expected to begin conforming to mission norms: early wakeups, chores, Bible studies, work in the Mission's thrift stores and kitchen, church attendance, and early curfew.

Of all the gospel rescue missions I researched nationwide, Grants Pass is the most severe. It is not a member of CityGate, but even if it were, I have yet to hear of any disciplinary process by which a mission could fall out of grace or membership. In chapter 9 you will hear the story of City Rescue Mission, which is a member of CityGate and had—under previous leadership—committed many of the same offenses, seemingly without any repercussions. My goal in sharing Sarah's experiences at Grants Pass is not to claim that they are the norm; rather, they illustrate what happens when the rescue mission's common practices and shared values are taken to their logical conclusion. As we explore these practices, we'll return often to Sarah's story, while also hearing from several others. Sarah's experience is certainly extreme in nature, but we must be clear that it is shared by many.

Most missions no longer flaunt harmful practices and language in the way Grants Pass does. But the flawed foundation—the belief that homelessness is a problem of sin solved only by faith in Jesus—remains. And the same ingredients continue to produce the same result: homelessness not being resolved, frequent exits from the program, and resistance to evidence-based practices that *do* end homelessness.

While missions vary in the vigor with which they hold these beliefs, the core principles are still largely consistent from mission to mission. We'll get a glimpse inside several gospel rescue missions from across the country through the experiences of staff, guests, and researchers. These testimonies affirm the institution's historical lineage we've established—that despite the independent structure and the freedom with which they operate, their differences are dwarfed by their similarities.

Gospel rescue missions do not own a monopoly on harmful values and practices. Viewing homelessness as a moral failure, expecting unhoused people to demonstrate their worthiness of housing through herculean efforts, and perpetuating unethical practices are problems that also exist in other ministries, secular nonprofits, and government programs. Rescue missions are simply the foremost example we have to interrogate these values—and the most vocal champion of these values' efficacy. We should resist and oppose harmful beliefs and behaviors wherever they arise, just as we should affirm and celebrate best practices wherever they are found—even in a gospel rescue mission.

* * *

Monroe Free began working at a rescue mission in Pensacola, Florida, as a night chaplain in the 1980s. One of the first things staff there told him was to not believe a word that the residents said; they were not to be trusted. This instruction confirmed and reinforced his implicit beliefs: "I assumed that everyone who came into the Rescue Mission was a pagan because they were poor." But over time, this belief system was gradually punctured by conversations with the residents.

As a chaplain, he routinely asked people, "Where does God fit in your story?," hoping it would lead to a conversion moment. Instead, he was shocked at how often the men would respond expressing deep faith and reliance on God. Through these experiences, Monroe fell in love with working with the unhoused, and he began to imagine ways of doing that differently than what he found in Pensacola.

When the executive director position opened at Knox Area Rescue Mission in Knoxville, Tennessee, Monroe jumped at the opportunity to apply, and he secured the job. One of his earliest experiences, with a participant named Charlie, helped solidify the type of mission he wanted to run.

Long before Monroe's arrival, Charlie had built a reputation for violent episodes when he drank. The severity of these episodes was such that not only had he been issued a lifetime ban, but the entire facility was to enter a full lockdown any time Charlie was spotted approaching. Believing that everyone deserves a second chance, Monroe went out and spoke to Charlie the next time he came near, even as his staff begged him not to. The conversation was uneventful; even quaint. Whenever Charlie would come by, Monroe would seek him out, building a relationship over time. As the two built mutual trust, Charlie was invited back into the Mission and even enrolled in its programs, achieving prolonged sobriety . . . that is, until he relapsed.

This time, thankfully, there was no violent tirade, but Charlie did walk out of the Mission. Monroe set out after him, eventually catching up to him in a parking lot. When Monroe called out to him, Charlie yelled back, "Why don't you just leave me alone? I'm nothing but an old drunk." It was a crystallizing moment for Monroe.

> Charlie's problem wasn't that he was an old drunk, but that he thought of himself as an old drunk. He was fulfilling his image of himself. And [I realized] that Christian ministry to him would be helping him change his image

> of himself. If he could move from seeing himself as a worthless old drunk, to a child of God, there would be a fundamental change.

In Monroe's seventeen years as executive director, he strived to create a mission where everyone who came through the Mission could see themselves, and one another, through the eyes of God. He identified the need for staff who weren't just Christians but who had professional training in social work, mental health, and addiction recovery. He hammered on the need to "value every person who comes through the door and see them as having enormous opportunity, given the right resources." Theirs was one of the first missions in the country to switch chapel attendance from mandatory to optional. They stopped measuring success by professions of faith and instead celebrated those who achieved stability.

But each new change came with resistance. Staff, board members, and donors felt that the mission was straying from its calling. Some were ultimately convinced by Monroe's perspective, but others would not come around. Initially supported by fellow leaders within the Association of Gospel Rescue Missions (AGRM), he nonetheless came to be increasingly regarded as the "liberal one" for his policy changes.

Eventually, Monroe had to acknowledge the reality: "I just couldn't maintain my integrity and stay in the rescue mission world." After he left, his replacement—who came from the world of prison ministry—undid nearly all of Monroe's changes. After consulting for a few years, Monroe found an organization that allowed him to live out his faith and empower families experiencing homelessness without condescending to them: Habitat for Humanity. "Jesus informs how we do things, but we don't use Jesus to draw any lines." Monroe served as the executive director of their Greenville, South Carolina, chapter for more than a decade before his recent retirement.

Reflecting on his rescue mission experience, Monroe has a lot to be proud of. He hopes to write a book one day and call it *Everything I Need to Know I Learned at the Rescue Mission.* But at the end of his long time there, he wasn't able to overcome the culture that labeled as lesser the folks he came to love. "My chief issue [with rescue missions] is really not even theological," Monroe clarified. "It's anthropological. It's our view of people. It's our view of men and women who are poor. We don't value them."

* * *

In early 2025, the monthly newsletter from the Grants Pass Gospel Rescue Mission included this note:

> We like to say things like, "homelessness can happen to anyone" and while there is some truth to that, what we shouldn't imply is that homelessness happens randomly. We might just as well say that STDs can happen to anyone, but we all realize that they are the result of a particular behavior. That's why these things simply don't happen to just anyone. They predictably follow behaviors that God's Word tells us to avoid. . . . The abundance of homeless in our nation is symptomatic of a larger and broader culture that is ignorant of God's instructions regarding the details of how to live and receive blessing."[1]

When Sarah stayed at the Grants Pass Gospel Rescue Mission in the 2010s, she understood exactly how the mission viewed her and felt its ramifications. The rigorous schedule, the draconian rules, the way she remembers the staff flaunting their comparative wealth and status—the message was clear to her. The guests at the Mission were broken and unwanted, and they needed to accept this about themselves if they were to have any chance of moving forward.

The Bible study and chapel leaders would say this outright: "We were told that we were there because we were bad women, and because nobody wanted us. I felt bad to my core and would leave chapel angry, ashamed, and hurt most days." As soon as the Mission permitted, she got a job and took as many shifts and overtime as they allowed. She wanted to spend every possible moment away from the Mission, and chapel especially. But the humiliation followed her everywhere. To justify all her time away from the Mission, her boss had to sign off on every single hour of work. As a result, all of her coworkers knew where she lived, and the accompanying stigma and probing questions meant that even away from the Mission she felt demeaned. Wherever she went—among the few places the Mission permitted her to go—she wore the scarlet letter of her homelessness and was treated accordingly.

While the myth that homelessness is the fault of the individual experiencing it goes well beyond gospel rescue missions—and even well beyond faith communities—when it is wielded in the name of religion, it can become especially pernicious. Prosperity gospel—the idea that God rewards with wealth and punishes with poverty—has always been convenient for those who are already wealthy (or at least not poor) to justify their relative social position. But however popular it may be, it fails not only to pass muster with Jesus and his good news for the poor, but also to hold up to data.

The unique stories of unhoused people and the data we collect about them counteract these beliefs in any number of ways, but the best argument comes from zooming out and viewing homelessness on a communal level. Homelessness is, after all, an issue that affects communities; yet not all communities are affected equally. If homelessness were the result of personal failure—the result of sin—then we would expect that homelessness would correlate to those factors. Greg Colburnn and Clayton Page Aldern published the results of a thorough study asking this precise question: How do we account for regional differences in homelessness rates? They tested a number of traditional "explanations" of homelessness, including substance use, mental illness, and poverty, to see if the rates of these phenomena correlated with homelessness in any meaningful way.

The results were clear: cities and counties that had higher rates of mental illness and/or substance use did not show a correlative increase in homelessness. When it came to poverty, there was actually an *inverse* relationship to homelessness: cities and counties with higher rates of poverty actually had *less* homelessness, and cities with higher affluence had more. This counterintuitive relationship becomes clear when we consider what are actually the single strongest predictors of homelessness rates in a given region: the affordability and availability of housing.

Countless studies have indicated that cost and vacancy rates are the only statistically significant causal factors for predicting homelessness. Bringing this back to the realm of theology, we can only understand homelessness as a failure—as a sin—in the sense that God calls us, collectively, to take care of the needs of our neighbors, and that we as communities have failed to do so. Worse, we have used God to blame that failure on those who are already hurting and told them that their salvation lies entirely in the act of professing Christ—the same Christ who commanded us to love our neighbors, clothe the naked, and feed the hungry as if we were serving Christ himself. The sin of homelessness is not individual laziness, promiscuity, or drunkenness, but individual and collective greed, inhospitality, and indifference.

The only thing that every person who experiences homelessness has in common is that they are without housing. The data concludes what is obvious and inherent to the definition of homelessness, and confirms that the attributes of housing, rather than the attributes of the individual, are to blame. Advocates understand that homelessness is not a personal failure, but a policy failure. For us Christians who have so long misunderstood this, often willfully, it is also a theological failure.

* * *

Sarah wasn't resistant to faith: "I don't hate religion, and have spent my share of time in churches, youth groups, Christian camps, etc. I have stayed curious my whole life, even if I do not identify as religious." But the amount of Christian practice required by the Grants Pass Gospel Rescue Mission would eclipse the weekly routine of even the most devout. Monday through Friday, Morning Bible study was at eight in the morning, and Evening Chapel at 5:15 p.m. On Sundays, they were required to go to a local church—"of their choice," so long as it was among those deemed by the Mission to be "Bible-believing." To prove they had actually attended, they had to bring back a copy of the day's church bulletin. On the monthly evaluation form used to determine whether a guest's stay would be extended, the first two criteria to consider were attendance at these required services.

Religious requirements were for so long the hallmark of gospel rescue missions, by design and with pride. But somewhere along the way, something changed. More and more rescue missions made chapel and Bible study optional to their guests, such that now the majority of rescue missions operate this way. The first mention of such a change I was able to locate comes from *Invisible Neighbors*, a 2015 book by John Ashmen, who served as CEO of AGRM/CityGate from 2007 to 2023. Ashmen writes, "At some missions, [chapel] attendance is required in order to obtain assistance, adding a touch of tough regimentation to the often non-structured schedules of the guest; at other missions, chapel is optional. It depends on the mission leaders' philosophy."[2]

Ashmen's tenure may have coincided with this shift in its most criticized practice, but his book makes it clear that the idea that people needed to fundamentally change to overcome homelessness was as resonant as ever. Ashmen's CityGate touted the Four Rs of what missions are about:

Rescue: Pulling people to safety from adverse conditions and from choices and habits that lead to damaged health and death.

Redemption: Presenting people with a gospel that is about life transformation in Jesus and the reclamation of His creation.

Rehabilitation: Helping people break the bonds of addiction and desperate behavior and experience a life of healing and wholeness.

Re-assimilation: Preparing people to dwell in community and to have meaningful roles that lead to stability and missional living.[3]

The Four Rs would bring about CityGate's Eight S's of life transformation, envisioned in a series of concentric circles with an arrow moving from the center and outward:

Saved > Sober > Stable > Schooled > Skilled > Secure > Settled > Serving[4]

Life transformation became the buzzword phrase for CityGate and its missions across North America. This language is ubiquitous across hundreds of rescue missions' websites. As missions were less inclined to require chapel attendance, they began instituting "life transformation programs" which purported to address homelessness at its root. Guests at the mission may not have been required to attend chapel before they ate or stayed the night, but if guests wanted to stay longer or get more resources, it was the life transformation programs that were now mandatory. While some of these might include life skills, AA/12 Step, GED classes, or workforce development, these types of groups were still dwarfed by the number of Bible studies offered.

In this way, gospel rescue missions got to have their cake and eat it too; they could truthfully report that they no longer required their guests to attend chapel or Bible study, while continuing to leverage ongoing insecurities to funnel them into programs that functioned similarly. In one such instance as recently as 2021, the Bay Area Rescue Mission in California only allowed guests to stay in the emergency shelter for thirty days before insisting they choose between entering the life transformation program or leaving the mission altogether. These missions can claim they are giving people choices, but people experience it more like an ultimatum: "choose" our religious program, or try your luck on the streets. The image may have changed, but the underlying values remain.

Beyond the theological and ethical ramifications of this approach, the practical results should not go unnamed. At scale, programs that put treatment first, with housing as the reward for a changed life—rather than putting housing first as the catalyst and basis for subsequent flourishing—do not successfully end homelessness. As researchers Marybeth Shinn and Jill Khadduri note in their book *In the Midst of Plenty*, "the data seem to show that the treatment-first programs did not change people so much as they sorted them into those permitted to come indoors and those relegated to the streets."[5] In other words, gospel rescue missions are not efficient at ending homelessness, but are proficient at deciding who among the unhoused is worthy and not—a metric that perpetuates homelessness further for the majority discarded.

The proven solution is to lead with housing and then surround with supportive services, known colloquially as Housing First. Rather than asking people to identify and make progress on goals as demanding as employment, education, sobriety, and health while still experiencing homelessness, this philosophy understands that a safe home is the springboard *into* stability. While many are suspicious about the scalability of this methodology, we have already seen it succeed on a national level. In 2008, Veterans Affairs, with bipartisan support, committed to utilizing Housing First approaches with homeless vets, combining front-end housing vouchers with supportive case management before, during, and after housing had been obtained. The result? Since 2010, veteran homelessness has decreased by 55 percent, even as homelessness on the whole has gone up. In 2023, when overall homelessness hit a record high, veteran homelessness hit a record low.[6]

Rescue missions view housing as the reward for life transformation—in fact, the Eight S's put it seventh, not first. But when housing is deprioritized, the likelihood that a person can end their homelessness plummets. And in the end, the blame usually goes to the individual—not the program—for that failure. Instead of scrutinizing the mission, the person is labelled as unworthy.

Worse, many mission leaders (including Ashmen) have spoken expressly against Housing First and other best practices and have even had success in reshaping policy to such ends. Former CEOs of Union Rescue Mission in Los Angeles (Andy Bales) and Orange County Rescue Mission (Jim Palmer) were vocal and influential in the politics of homelessness in Southern California, where Housing First was implemented in name only but never invested in with an adequate supply of affordable housing. Bales, Palmer, and many other Christian leaders were quick to blame Housing First as a policy rather than its implementation, arguing instead that the mission's approach—mandating personal transformation prior to receiving life-saving resources—should once again become the national homelessness strategy. Rather than distinguishing themselves as a Christian alternative, gospel rescue missions under Ashmen's tenure touted their treatment-first method as *the* solution to end homelessness.

After a year at the Grants Pass Gospel Rescue Mission, Sarah was unceremoniously exited. She recalls no conversations or infractions that could have led to this dismissal. Devastated and with nowhere to go, she spiraled back into the same state she was in before the mission: relapsing into opioid use and couch-hopping amongst those who didn't have her best interests at heart. It wasn't until months later that she finally connected with a provider that met her actual, tangible needs. With the support of Options of Southern Oregon, she suddenly experienced all that she'd needed the whole time but was never offered by the mission, and it gave her the confidence and capacity to put her life back together.

> All of these supports led to me feeling strong, worthy and capable. Therapy, advocacy, addiction support, medication support, employment guidance, stable housing. Wraparound care. Healing truly does begin when a person feels they have a safe home to sleep in. I tried to heal for years, but the true healing did not begin until I had a safe home to call my own.

Rather than working to provide what Sarah needed—and deserved—the Grants Pass Mission made every effort to convince Sarah that she was unworthy of having these needs met unless and until she believed in their Jesus. It's a twisted irony that this had the opposite effect: "Living at the Mission definitely turned me further away from any ideas of following an organized religion. It made religion feel unsafe and judgmental, in very unhealthy ways . . . I am still angry with the Chapel program and have not been back to church since leaving the mission."

* * *

It had been an especially cold and dreary night in Portland, Oregon. Having hardly slept a wink, Gus Kroll and a few dozen other unhoused folks stood outside the Portland Rescue Mission, eagerly awaiting the facility's early opening time. The doors eventually opened, and they shuffled into the chapel to find their seats. They knew that before they would be allowed to eat, they would have to "sing for their supper." But this particular morning, they had an especially hard time staying awake.

The warmth of the chapel, the exhaustion, and the same old judgmental sermon left the entire audience nearly catatonic. One older man had the misfortune of falling asleep first. The staff noticed immediately and escorted the man out. They sent him, Gus remembers with disgust, "out on his ear, out in the cold with nothing to eat and nowhere warm to go." For the rest of the service, everyone was at full attention.

Gus doesn't remember the sermon at all. But he remembers that old man, whose only crime was falling asleep in a warm place after a cold, restless night. Moreover, Gus remembers how powerless he felt in the face of such injustice: "They should have had a riot on their hands, but instead we all just watched. . . . No one was willing to risk their own breakfast to say it is wrong for you to be throwing an exhausted and hungry man out without breakfast and you should be ashamed of yourselves." It's no surprise that Gus has spent his career since working with unhoused people in Portland, drawn especially to those often discarded even by other service providers.

On the other side of the country, and from the other side of the pulpit, Dennis Edwards took note of a similar injustice. Long before his PhD would make him "Dr. Edwards," he was a young soon-to-be seminarian looking for preaching experience. His pastor suggested he preach at the nearby gospel rescue mission—none other than the McAuley Water Street Mission, the one that started it all. Edwards was paired with another parishioner and a retired missionary to lead a regular chapel service where he would preach.

He took it for granted that the men had to sit through his service before eating—that's just the way it is, he thought. When people fell asleep or seemed distracted, he assumed it was because he wasn't being engaging enough—perhaps this was why he needed preaching experience! In part, he grappled with the style of preaching he was asked to do: "Every church service was like a mini–Billy Graham crusade. You had to get an altar call." Eventually it set in for him that the structure of making people sit through the sermon was the problem, and that the assumptions inherent to that design were at odds with the compassion he felt for the men.

His fellow parishioner, though, did not see it that way. Edwards remembers him constantly degrading the men, both behind their backs and to their faces. On the drive into New York City every month, Edwards and the retired missionary would admire the city's beauty, but their carmate would simply say, "It's Sodom," a biblical euphemism for a city plagued by wickedness and deserving of God's destruction. One particular night, Edwards recalls that they opened up the chapel service to testimonies from the men, and an individual came forward to share that he had just been released from prison earlier that day. Before he could continue, the parishioner interrupted to imply that this man must have spent the day seeking out the services of a sex worker. The man responded that he had not, but rather had spent the whole day wandering the city trying to figure out what he was going to do with his life. A switch flipped in Edwards, and he realized he could no longer tolerate the viewpoint of his fellow volunteer and the many ways this viewpoint reflected those of the program. He continued preaching there, however, not wanting to abandon the men, but trying in his messages to subtly subvert the judgment they were accustomed to. Then he went away for seminary.

After graduating, Edwards returned to New York to plant a church. He also returned to McAuley's mission, signing up to lead a monthly service—but with a new approach and some new back-up. Specifically, he brought members from his church plant, instilled with a different sense than Edwards' previous company of what they were there to do:

> We saw ourselves as trying to offer some kind of a gift. We thought the space that we occupy is this church space for them. So let's just be some kind of spiritual encouragement there. We're not going to make them our target. We'll make them our community for the night.

When Edwards moved his ministry to the nation's capital, he was invited to lead Bible study and preach in chapel at Gospel Rescue Ministries of Washington, DC. There, he encountered an environment much more suited to his style. The leader, Edward Eyring, instilled practices that conferred humanity and dignity to the residents, and all of the Bible studies and chapel services that Edwards spoke at were optional.

Like Gus, Edwards was shaped by his time in the mission in a way that reverberates in his current work. In one of his many books, Edwards pronounces, "The power of the gospel is often most visible among those who have been the least respected."[7] As a New Testament professor and now dean of North Park Theological Seminary in Chicago, he instills this "gospel from the margins" into generations of students. Gus and Edwards both became who they are in part through confrontation with the gospel of the rescue mission, and each found new ways to live out the values they sharpened after experiencing its worst qualities.

* * *

In nearly every gospel rescue mission story I heard, there was at least one shocking anecdote. This forced me to ask what it could be that made these missions so prone to the outrageous. Sarah's story alone contained many such instances: Bible study leaders using their lessons to teach flat-earth theories as biblical truth; discovering her bed was mold-ridden, only to be threatened with discharge for reporting it as this "made the Mission look bad"; guests surveilled by staff and their "eyes" in the community, reporting such menial rule infractions as smoking a cigarette across town.

While the stories themselves are appalling, they point to a structural feature of gospel rescue missions that make such stories possible, if not common. All nonprofits, including rescue missions, are required to have a board of directors, but because each mission is an independent entity, they don't report to CityGate or to any denominational structure. This allows individual missions to be largely self-contained, further protected by the powerlessness of their clients and the ignorance of their donors. As a result of this insulation, the theology at work in these institutions is often far more extreme than advertised, and operational misconduct can go unaddressed.

Gospel rescue missions are explicitly evangelical in their theology, but there's no formal limit on how stringent this theology can be. At the Grants Pass Gospel Rescue Mission, another Bible study teacher informed the women that if any of them had previously undergone an abortion, the fetuses were assuredly burning in hell. At Knox Area Rescue Mission, Monroe Free lost donors when he strayed from exclusive use of the King James Version of the Bible. Multiple mission staff at different locations across the country recounted tense exchanges about which atonement theory they ascribed to.

Margaret Vorih, who worked at the Capital City Rescue Mission in Albany, New York, was in her early sixties and grappling with a worsening chronic health condition when the COVID-19 pandemic struck. When she approached leadership about whether her coworkers would be masking, if air purifiers would be purchased, and what accommodations she could count on for her own safety and that of her staff, her trust in God was called into question. When her home church remained closed for in-person worship longer than most, she was pressured to worship elsewhere to fulfill the staff covenant's mandate of regular church participation. The fact that Margaret's regular church engagement took place virtually was deemed unacceptable to the Rescue Mission's leadership. Gradually, and painfully, she was compelled to move on.

These extreme philosophies operate in part because they aren't subject to independent oversight, something most homelessness nonprofits receive from governmental agencies in the form of monitoring and inspections. While governmental oversight is by no means the gold standard, it at least provides a base level of independent accountability. For their part, gospel rescue missions have largely declined government funding in order to protect against what they perceive as political agendas antithetical to their objectives. Some are even so antagonistic toward government programs that they won't allow their guests to sign up for benefits like food stamps or social security, as was the case when Margaret was at Capital City.

Ultimately, any organization is subject to the oversight of its funders. In the case of gospel rescue missions, however, the vast majority of funding comes from churches and individual Christian donors. These donors have little knowledge of the inner workings of their local gospel rescue mission—what rules govern the lives of the guests, what aberrant theologies take root, and what outcomes are produced. This allows the gospel rescue missions to run as they see fit while projecting whatever image best suits their donor base.

In his research on rescue missions, Ronald Fagan observed that, for those who support financially and by volunteering, "The missions allow them to minister to a 'needy' population within a relatively safe, nonthreatening environment."[8] He also recognizes another, much more significant group, one that doesn't directly interact with the mission at all except through the distribution of newsletters: "None of the newsletters we evaluated contained any data that indicated an overall success rate. The only data that were reported were total numbers of people served. It would appear that the supporters do not demand more than this type of information."[9]

Lyndsie Francis, who worked at the Bay Area Rescue Mission in volunteer and donor relations, echoed these same realities nearly forty years after Fagan:

> The thing I learned about volunteerism is that most people are just looking for an opportunity to feel good. . . . It seemed to me that most churches in the area were more interested in writing big checks, and maybe having a plaque on the wall with their name on it, than getting more deeply involved and actually meeting the needs of the Mission.

To be sure, there are plenty of Christians and churches donating to gospel rescue missions so that they will do *precisely* these things, and who would not be dissuaded by any of the stories or arguments above. However, for Christians who develop a heart toward the issue of homelessness and wish to volunteer or donate, gospel rescue missions are very often the first or only known option to receive these resources.

As we shift our focus toward different models of ministry, I hope it becomes clear that, despite their central and vocal position in numerous communities, gospel rescue missions do not define the Christian landscape of homelessness work. The organizations we will encounter represent only a fraction of those doing incredible work, fueled and enriched by a deep faith that honors the image of God in every person.

If gospel rescue missions are to transform their ways of thought and practice, it will be because those who support them expect that change to happen. In hope for that change, we will spend time learning from organizations that embody a different set of values, values that also produce a more transformative set of outcomes. For Christians looking to support ministries faithfully ending homelessness, the following chapters provide not just a sizable list of worthy options, but qualities to look for when discerning whether to support an organization in your area. In them you may find a roadmap to follow, or perhaps just a kernel of an idea to bring to your context. In all of them, I hope you will find a worthy response to the call to end homelessness.

THREE

Building Housing for Good

Calvary Lutheran Church—Minneapolis, MN

Heart of the Rockies Christian Church—Fort Collins, CO

Caldwell Presbyterian Church—Charlotte, NC

The question is not whether the church is dying, but whether it is giving its life for the world." In these uncertain times of church decline in the West, these words from the late Fred Craddock are perhaps more relevant than ever.

In the late 1940s, Gallup research showed that nearly 80 percent of Americans claimed to belong to a house of worship. In 2024, that number is only 45 percent. It is far outside the scope of this book to wade into the fraught debates about why that is, or what could change it. This is not about whether the church (writ large) will survive, or how. What seems unavoidable, though, is that churches will increasingly face difficult decisions in response to these trends, particularly around real estate. The long-term future of the church is an open question, but the immediate future of many individual churches is hanging heavy on the hearts of pastors and church boards across the country *right now*.

As churches wonder what to do with so much real estate, millions of Americans at or below the poverty line are running out of places they can afford to live. For every one hundred households in America considered extremely low income, there are only thirty affordable and available rentals. To meet this immense need, we would need 7.1 million affordable homes added to our housing stock. The housing affordability crisis, as we've explored, is the primary driver of homelessness. Increasing the availability of affordable housing must be our North Star, even as we triage the more immediate needs of those unhoused and at-risk.

In the midst of these crises, many churches have explored using their property in a variety of creative, Spirit-led ways to provide housing to their unhoused neighbors. The three churches we will highlight here were all at different places in their congregational life: one nearing closure, one experiencing a revival, and one maintaining a steady, healthy membership for thirty years. While they've each had differing experiences of the existential crisis of church decline, they all saw the external crisis of affordable housing and chose to leverage their own futures to meet it.

These offerings ought to be considered as non-exhaustive options; they might be a blueprint, or they might be imaginative kindling for your own unique idea. Whatever form our response takes, I believe these two things are true: (1) tens of thousands of churches will close or be forced to restructure in America and Canada in the next decade, and (2) affordable housing is one of the most impactful uses of church property to serve the neighborhood.

Pastor and professor Mark DeYmaz says it cleverly and decidedly: "Pastors and churches can no longer afford to sit on their assets."[1] We can choose to fight this changing reality as though it means the death of the church, or perhaps understand it as a fresh movement of the Spirit.

* * *

At the corner of 39th Street and Chicago Avenue in Minneapolis, Minnesota, a large steeple overlooks the neighborhood. Adorning this steeple is a mural of the face of George Floyd, the South Minneapolis resident who was murdered by police on May 21, 2020. The mural was designed by Ella Endo, a high-schooler and church member of Calvary Lutheran, to whom the steeple belongs. The piece features Floyd's face in black and white, the negative space of which is filled with words that his friends and family members used to describe him.

This mural is a fixture of the community space known as George Floyd Square, centered on 38th Street and Chicago Avenue where Floyd was killed, and extending a block in each direction. The site has become a center for community gathering, organizing, and mutual aid. When you drive through it, you immediately become aware of how the community has claimed this zone. Each outpost is a four-way stop, the signage prominently installed in the median of the intersection; street art, flowers, and protest signs embellish and inject it with meaning; a bus-stop-turned-clothing-closet, free library, and food pantry resource the neighborhood. As thousands of commuters drive through this prominent intersection daily, they reckon not only with the injustice of Floyd's death, but with the community's radical insistence on a better way of life.

For Calvary Lutheran Church, Floyd's murder in the midst of the COVID-19 pandemic solidified their desire to stay on the southernmost corner of George Floyd Square. Thirty years prior, a church event inspired the coining of their signature phrase: "In this city for good"—a play on words indicating not only the church's plans to endure but also their posture for how they would *be* in the city. When national attention came to the corner of 38th and Chicago, however, the "city" shrank, and they recognized their calling was more specific.

Josh and Joani Moberg were leaders in the church's effort to determine their future. When I asked Josh about their proximity to George Floyd Square, he said, "We really felt ever more strongly this calling to be rooted on 39th Street and Chicago Avenue, to this specific intersection, this specific building. People saw us, and they recognized the congregation as a good neighbor."

Their ability to endure as a church, regardless of their neighborhood posture, had been in question for decades. In the 90s, Calvary was on the brink of closing before a large estate donation from a recently deceased church member gave them new life. The donation bought them twenty years to keep worshiping and loving their community. They started the Urban Arts Academy to provide holistic art education to preschool, elementary, and middle school students;

and they operated one of the largest food pantries in South Minneapolis. But while they thrived missionally, their congregation gradually dwindled, and their underutilized buildings aged and required more and more restoration and repair.

Around 2017, Calvary determined that they had less than five years before their blessing would run out. Joani, who had been a member of Calvary for fifty years, chaired the Sustainable Calvary Steering Committee to survey their facilities and look for challenges and opportunities, all of which would be included in a report and presented to the church council. They hoped, of course, to find a way to save their congregation, to indeed remain there "for good," but only so long as they could uphold both ends of the double entendre. Joani's ethos was clear: "Let's make sure we're not saving this congregation just for the sake of it. Let's make sure that we're all in agreement that the reason we're saving this congregation is because we have something worth saving because we have something to offer to our community."

The next year, Joani and her team presented their findings: there was no path to sustainability that didn't include a sale of at least part of their property.

In the ensuing years, they left no stone unturned. They knew they wouldn't sell just to sell—there had to be missional alignment. They considered merging with another church so that one property could be sold and the other could be sustained. They looked at selling only the parking lot, or only the education building. After many fits and starts, an opportunity arose that at first seemed terrifying but eventually grew on them.

They could sell the entire property to an affordable housing developer called Trellis, who would convert nearly every square inch into the Belfry Apartments: forty-one units, and a community room where the sanctuary stood.

In one early conversation, it seemed that Trellis might have to demolish the entirety of the building in order to move forward. The congregation, led by the church council and the steering committee, began engaging the possibility. Affordable housing was an easy missional fit, but there was of course hope that the church's sanctuary could remain untouched and in their ownership if possible.

But when it became clear that wouldn't be possible, Calvary was ready. Joani remembers standing before the congregation with the steering committee's recommendation to sell the building, saying, "The people and the mission are the most important thing here, not the building. I love this building, but I love the people more. And if the wrecking ball has to swing for this congregation to continue, I will stand outside and I will watch it, because that's how important you are to me."

Joani and Josh, who led the church council at the time, both attribute a lot of what came next to the unique crises of 2020. The COVID-19 pandemic required that Calvary, and every other church, imagine what church community and worship could be beyond meeting in a building, easing their anxieties and questions about a sale or even a potential demolition. And the murder of George Floyd reminded them of their unique calling and rootedness in the corner of 39th and Chicago, dispelling any thoughts of relocating or merging into another church's building. When the church finally voted on the intent to sell to Trellis in April of the next year, the vote was unanimous.

The collaboration between Calvary and Trellis was one of partnership and reciprocity. Trellis had their own vision for mostly single units, but Calvary knew their neighborhood. Largely comprised of families with longtime roots who faced increasing risk that they'd be priced out by gentrification, the neighborhood needed multiroom units more than singles. The church council made a request that this be prioritized, which Trellis honored. When the parking lot area was razed for a new construction comprising twenty-one units, and the education wing converted to another twenty, the rental mix included a variety of unit sizes that reflect the diverse population and needs of the immediate neighborhood.

As part of the agreement to sell the entire property, Calvary was the first renter—not of one of the apartments, but of the new community room. During the construction, Trellis secured some funding to preserve aspects of the original architecture as a historical monument; namely, the ornate vestiges of the historic sanctuary. But it was important to both Trellis and Calvary for the room to serve a function not just for the church but for the new residents. The result is one of the most fascinating spaces I've ever seen.

The community-center-slash-sanctuary is a true mash-up of styles. The chancel (where the pulpit, baptismal font, and altars are placed) remains in its original wood at the front of the room. The historic stained glass windows, newly repaired, still diffuse sunlight into the space, dappling it with color. The rest of the room, however, has been transformed. The floors are laminate and leveled—previously, a steep slope graded the floor. What was the seating area of the sanctuary can now be flexibly rearranged as a formal worship space or a communal, social one. A coffee counter extends the social invitation of the new space, and brand-new air conditioning is a welcome upgrade. This strange amalgamation is rented on Sundays by Calvary, and the rest of the week serves as a gathering, activity, and relaxation space for the residents of the Belfry Apartments.

And so, Calvary Church remains as a congregation in an entirely unexpected way, with the burden of a dilapidated building no longer dragging their finances or anxieties. Their presence on the corner of 39th and Chicago endures, their food pantry and participation in George Floyd Square continuing strong. Forty-one new, deeply affordable apartments have opened in a neighborhood that desperately needed them. Whether or not Calvary is still worshiping in fifty years, the apartments stand to house families and individuals for generations.

Rev. Diane Moffett, president and executive director of the Presbyterian Mission Agency, once said, "My question is whether churches are willing to birth something new that reflects the principles of the kingdom. Can you leave something that generations from now people will see and say it makes the community better?"[2] In one way or another, Calvary has cemented that they will be in the city—in their neighborhood—for good.

* * *

Toward the end of the twentieth century, Fort Collins, Colorado was growing rapidly. From 1980 to 2000, as the population nearly doubled, the city expanded and developed further south to accommodate. Amid this expansion, the Central Rocky Mountain Region of the Christian Church (Disciples of Christ) identified Fort Collins for a second church plant to meet the spiritual needs of a growing city. They called a pastor and purchased eleven acres of pastureland in 1993.

From the outset, this new congregation, called Heart of the Rockies Christian Church, decided that the eleven acres would be for more than just the church building. As they began to form, they divided the land into two distinct plots: two and a half acres would be developed for their church facilities, and the remainder would be set aside for a future vision—one that would serve the community.

The first real attempt at a vision project came in 2006: a campus for nonprofits focused on children and families called SKYhill. Years into the church's planning and conversations, though, the city of Fort Collins poured funding into a similar project that met most of the needs that SKYhill had hoped to address. SKYhill no longer felt pertinent, especially in light of the 2008 recession.

When Rev. Melissa St. Clair succeeded the founding pastor in 2012, she inherited and reaffirmed this hope. Two years later, one of the initial partners for SKYhill approached Heart of the Rockies to restart the conversation, and excitement was rekindled. In the end, though, they could not come to a cohesive vision around the project, and it was once again in danger of a prolonged hibernation.

Instead, leadership made a critical series of decisions. First, they decided to officially "let go" of the SKYhill project. This was a difficult choice given the years of work and hope invested. Melissa, through her own prayer and discernment, recognized that to be truly faithful to the day-to-day responsibilities of her role, the project would require a driving force from within the congregation to spearhead it. She and Stacy Poncelow, the board moderator at the time, approached two women in the congregation to be co-leaders. One of them was Cristina Mahon, a senior leader at Hewlett

Packard with decades of project management experience, who now serves as board moderator and is the primary spokesperson for the church and its projects. Lastly, a clarifying word from Stacy set a new tone: they were surrendering *this* vision for the nearly nine acres, but they could maintain the momentum and dreams of the congregation by opening themselves to a new vision rather than giving up altogether.

The vision has always been broader than helping kids and youth; it was about how the church could be a partner in whatever may be best for the community. Heart of the Rockies wanted to be in neighboring relationships with whoever would come to use the land—not to increase church attendance, but to deepen community with the neighborhood. This hope was further reinforced by a Disciples of Christ outreach initiative called Be the Neighbor, which promotes doing justice and mission work in a way that is relational, sustainable, and dignity-affirming. Cristina summarizes the approach as "doing things *with* folks, not doing things *to* folks." At every juncture, the congregation wanted more than anything to have a campus marked by community.

Cristina describes this period as when they truly surrendered the project to God. The church began referring to it as "The Next Big Thing" instead of "SKYhill" to open themselves up to whatever might come. As 2020 approached, Heart of the Rockies released a request for proposals (RFP) to the community to find out what they would want to do with the land in partnership with the church. They had little sense of whether they would get any proposals at all, much less if any would be viable or match their vision. When COVID-19 emerged prior to the RFP deadline, the church increasingly thought that nothing would come of this effort, and that it would only serve as a learning opportunity for their next attempt.

Instead, they received nine proposals. Several, from for-profit developers looking to capitalize, they dismissed outright. A couple others they looked into and decided didn't align with their values. Three proposals remained: one from CARE Communities (a local nonprofit) to develop affordable housing units, one from Fort Collins Habitat for Humanity to develop single-family homes, and one from L'Arche Northern Colorado to develop housing for adults with intellectual disabilities. All three aligned critically with the church's mission as well as with each other. Heart of the Rockies decided to pursue all three as a joint collaborative project.

CARE Communities, which had the capital and capacity to break ground quickly, took the lead. Melissa remembers what a seamless fit it was right from the beginning—that CARE understood their desire to "create synergy, to collaborate, to be something greater together than we could be individually." When the church shared their ideas for inviting their future neighbors to activities and classes, CARE Communities trusted them enough to know they weren't out to proselytize. The congregation could see the fulfillment of every hope and dream they had harbored for decades.

The project gained momentum quickly, in no small part because of what Melissa refers to as "the generativity of generosity." The church donated the land to CARE Communities to begin "horizontal" development (the development of land in the form of grading, foundation, and utilities needed before construction of edifices can begin). Rather than only doing this stage of development for their part of the project, CARE did the entire parcel, then sold the lots Habitat needed for the single-family homes to them at cost, speeding up their process and allowing Habitat to lean into their strengths as an organization. Habitat, paying that generosity forward, offered to purchase the two lots for L'Arche if they weren't able to raise enough funds in time. Melissa and Heart of the Rockies could only marvel at the ways one gift begat another and another.

For decades to come, this generative generosity will be generational. In the end, eight and a half acres of pastureland became seventy-two units of affordable rental housing of various family sizes (CARE Communities), nine single-family homes to be owned by their occupants (Habitat for Humanity), and two houses for adults with intellectual disabilities to share (L'Arche). For all partners to share, the church included, there is new greenspace, a community garden, a playground, an outdoor gathering space, and a community center. They have hopes for an early childhood education center to come later; a nod, perhaps, to the original SKYhill vision.

The project, now known as Heartside Hill, began opening its doors to its new residents in 2025. Both Cristina and Melissa hope that the project inspires more churches in Fort Collins and beyond to generosity, and to be a living example of the call to love God and neighbor.

* * *

In his book *Building Belonging: The Church's Call to Build Community and House Our Neighbors*, Rev. John Cleghorn tells the stories of dozens of churches across the country who have built affordable housing on their property. He rightly sees this not as a fleeting phenomenon, but a growing movement, still in its infancy, that has the capacity to bring new life to the church in America.

But Rev. Cleghorn is more than a simple observer or even champion of this trend. He is a practitioner, alongside Caldwell Presbyterian Church, which he leads—and their story is an incredible one.

John, who spent twenty-five years in journalism and banking, was called by Caldwell Presbyterian Church in Charlotte, North Carolina, to serve as their pastor in 2008. Two years prior, the congregation had actually voted to close the church when something unexpected happened: A group of young, active Christians who had been meeting together but did not belong to a church body decided to visit, and they loved their experience. Quickly, the church entered a renewal, one that Cleghorn inherited in its early stages and stewarded forward. The congregation numbered over three hundred within a few years as they together pursued "a social-justice-oriented mission" and a worship style John describes as "familiar to longtime Presbyterians and other Protestants, but more relaxed and even joyful."

In 2013, Caldwell Presbyterian was celebrating one hundred years in the community. The goal of acknowledging its centennial was both to look to the past and cast a vision for the future. Little did they know that these two would collide in unexpected, and even shocking, ways.

In their study of the past, they discovered where the name *Caldwell* came from. In 1922, the last remaining member of the Caldwell family donated a fortune to what had previously been called John Knox Presbyterian. The congregation changed their name to honor the gift and remained Caldwell Memorial Presbyterian for the next century. When a dutiful elder looked up the Caldwells, she was dismayed to discover the source of their immense wealth: they owned and operated a plantation that profited on the labor of dozens of slaves.

As they read through the names of the humans who generated the Caldwells' wealth—which the church used to build its beautiful sanctuary—one name stood out: Easter. As a church that had recently faced the possibility of closure before experiencing their own "resurrection," the word *Easter* was often on their lips. The name now had a more complex meaning—holding the shame of the past and the responsibility for a new future.

After the centennial, the church pitched ideas for what they wanted to take on as part of their "next hundred years," and one idea kept reemerging: housing. A few years before, they had opened a floor of the building next door—an unused and underkept education edifice—to operate as emergency shelter for fifty women experiencing homelessness. Their original commitment was for sixty days, but the shelter remained open for three and half years as homelessness grew. These years were full of joys, challenges, and lessons learned—but most importantly, the solidifying of a calling.

Having been engaged in antiracist work, Caldwell knows well that the crises of racism and homelessness are deeply intertwined. While Black people make up 13 percent of the U.S. population, they account for 37 percent of those experiencing homelessness. Anti-Black racism entrenched in historic and present policies and practices presses Black Americans to the margins of social and economic participation while simultaneously barricading their reentry. As Kara Young Ponder, director of community engagement and racial justice at the UCSF Benioff Homelessness and Housing Initiative, explains, "Structural, institutional and interpersonal racism in our housing, criminal justice and education systems mean that Black Americans disproportionately struggle to find consistent housing, are vulnerable to displacement into homelessness and face more barriers when trying to get rehoused."[3]

While these realities exist nationwide, they are felt uniquely in Charlotte at this confluence of race, housing, and church. In his book *Our Trespasses: White Churches and the Taking of American Neighborhoods*, author and organizer Greg Jarrell documents Charlotte's sordid history around displacement and the destruction of Black neighborhoods—particularly the predominantly Black neighborhood of Brooklyn—and the long-term ramifications on racial disparities in present-day Charlotte.[4] Especially of note is the way churches in Charlotte were complicit in the eradication of a historically Black neighborhood in Brooklyn to the benefit of Charlotte's wealthy white residents. From Charlotte First Baptist Church's winning of a significant portion of land in an auction, to the documented conspiring of multiple pastors to baptize the city's effort in spiritual language of cleansing and renewal—the historic white Christian landscape of Charlotte, North Carolina has a lot to answer for.

With this robust understanding of the issues affecting Charlotte, Caldwell Presbyterian developed their vision of twenty-one permanent supportive studio apartments for people coming out of chronic homelessness. They partnered with a local homelessness nonprofit, Roof Above, which committed to providing the necessary supportive services. They found another willing collaborator in DreamKey Partners, a nonprofit housing developer. And they chose a fitting name: Easter's Home.

Such a project takes years of development, and Caldwell spent those years committed to learning and preparing themselves to be the best possible neighbors to the future residents of Easter's Home. In that time, they did several book studies, invited local and national speakers, and preached consistently on the project on Sunday mornings—truly an all-encompassing effort to make Easter's Home a core part of their identity, and to dedicate themselves to the nuances of doing it *right*.

As of the time of writing, Easter's Home hopes to open by the end of 2025. While the work of repair in the community of Charlotte remains unfinished, the project signals to the community that these followers of Jesus will reject the way of the Caldwells and will instead align themselves with the destiny of the Easters of this world.

* * *

I had the opportunity to visit and preach at Caldwell Presbyterian Church in the spring of 2023. I got to see and experience the great things they were up to and offer insights and encouragements. I preached that morning on Matthew 25, where Jesus says that when we feed the hungry, clothe the naked, and visit the imprisoned, we are not just meeting those individuals but are in fact meeting Christ himself. My message suggested that in these encounters, if we truly believed that we were interacting with Jesus, our approach would be more than transactional or unidirectional. If we believed that every unhoused person we encounter is Jesus, we would not only want to help them; we would also want to sit with them, learn from them, and be transformed by them.

That morning, a woman from the congregation had been asked to be the liturgist. Throughout the service, she read scriptures and prayers and, after my sermon, was set to come up and give some announcements. Before she did so, however, she shared something with the congregation: thirty days ago, she and her three sons had received a thirty-day notice to vacate, and they were scrambling to find a place to live. She cried as she admitted to the congregation that she was nearing homelessness—something she had experienced before—if something didn't change. She commented on the sermon, emphasizing that homelessness is not merely the experience of "those people" out there, but a crisis impinging on someone in their very midst, and likely others. She had been guarding that hardship from others—until that morning.

She opened and closed her story by sharing an expression she had learned from her grandmother: "Tell the truth and shame the devil." For her, this meant that it was important that morning to share the reality of her situation, difficult as it was, to reveal the way that shame and pride shield us from the experiences of oppression and hardship of our immediate neighbors and friends. Homelessness—a social evil—thrives when we allow shame, fear, or myths to prevent us from talking about it openly and honestly. While my sermon confronted some of these realities, her decision to open a fresh wound in front of her community transformed that shame and fear into power and possibility. The congregation immediately took a separate offering just for her. I didn't hear the total raised, but I got a view from the stage of the church's generosity—and having spent time with them, I'm certain this was the beginning, not the end, of their support for her.

Reflecting on this experience, I know that it wasn't my sermon that elicited this moment. Allowing me to preach on homelessness was one small blip in a years-long posture of openness that this congregation had embraced toward the unhoused in their community. My message to them to be transformed by their encounters with their neighbors served not as a challenge, but a reminder of what they were already doing. In this openness, and in the courageous revelation from one of their own, the congregation left that morning with a fresh truth: following Jesus on the mission to end homelessness may begin with a mission to serve others, but it ends when the distinction between *us* and *them* falls away, and we are all brought into community and wholeness together.

When we tell that truth, the devil doesn't stand a chance.

Go and do likewise

The effort to convert church land into affordable housing is one of the biggest and most exciting faith movements related to homelessness in the world right now. It is one of the most urgent and emergent ways the church can answer the question, "Where has God given us abundance to meet the scarcity of our neighborhood?"

This conversation need not be reserved for those who are shuttering churches; as we've seen, churches that are thriving, surviving, or somewhere in the middle have responded to this opportunity in their own unique ways. Any Christian community that stewards space or property can and ought to be imagining ways to maximize these resources to the benefit of others.

A common thread among those churches highlighted is a spirit of openness. The decision to open doors requires first an opening of hearts to shared life and destiny with neighbors; discomfort and conflict are inherent byproducts of any authentic relationship and should be met with humility. Calvary, Heart of the Rockies, and Caldwell all see themselves in a partnership with the needs, desires, experiences, and futures of those who find their home among them.

This openness doesn't just follow the decision; it precedes it. Every story recounted here involves years and years of preparation: commitment to learning, to cultivating an understanding of social justice, to faithful presence in the neighborhood, and to a long-term project that will necessarily morph and complicate over time. In order to do the big thing, these folks had to be faithful in all of the small ways for years, even decades. If your community feels far from embarking on such a significant project, know that every conversation, every sermon, every meeting is a brick laid in the foundation for whatever work God may have in store when the time is right.

In each story, key partnerships were crucial to success. While these churches each recognized the value that they could bring in terms of infrastructure and a commitment to Christian neighborliness, they also knew that they were not experts in housing development, construction, or service provision. It would have been easier, and cheaper perhaps, for these churches to insist on over-involvement in these areas. Instead, after vetting their partners for shared values and commitments, they humbly allowed development and supportive service partners to do what they do best.

Such openness, humility, and vulnerability can perhaps best be summed up as *faith*. The church in America will need this same faith to navigate the tumultuous times that we've now inherited. In all this, I'm reminded of the refrain that "the church is not a building, it's a people." As we continue along this trajectory where formal membership declines and the resources we steward go underutilized, we have an incredible opportunity to meet the housing needs of our communities with how we go about closing, moving, or sustaining our churches. While many churches hope for a revival that will bring us back to days gone by, I am convinced that this *is* the revival. This is the moment where the church is called back to its identity as followers of a peculiar way of loving neighbors more than its traditions, its history, and its property; a church that is willing to live, and even die, for the sake of others.

FOUR

Confronting Housing Policy, Proliferating Housing

Beacon Interfaith Housing Collaborative—Minneapolis, MN

Firm Foundation Community Housing—Hayward, CA

In this book, I could only share a fraction of the stories I've heard from congregations committed to building housing. But a throughline across every one was resistance from the churches' surrounding communities. Operating under the myth that affordable housing increases crime and decreases property values, neighbors often vehemently oppose these types of projects. This phenomenon, known as NIMBYism ("not in my backyard"), emerges over and over again in these stories as neighbors prioritize their own desires regarding the socioeconomic makeup of their neighborhoods over the housing needs of the broader community.

But only one story involved a giant inflatable Godzilla.

That story belongs to Plymouth Congregational Church, an affluent church in Minneapolis that had purchased an abandoned nursing home across the street from its campus. Dubbing it Lydia Apartments, they had begun converting it to permanent supportive housing for people exiting homelessness. Resistance was fierce: The church was picketed every Sunday by dozens of protesters for an entire year; the church and its board were sued; a church leader's *wedding* was picketed. The aforementioned blow-up reptile, pitched on the roof of a neighboring building, was accompanied by an enormous sign reading "Lydia Apartments—A Monster of an Idea."

But the resistance backfired. The church galvanized so emphatically around the mission to open Lydia Apartments that it became core to their identity. Parts of the city that might have otherwise never even heard about the project rallied in support. The development became a differentiating topic in the Minneapolis mayoral race. In the end, Lydia Apartments opened; and then Nicollet Square, Creekside Commons, and a dozen more similar housing complexes. The Plymouth Church Neighborhood Foundation, tasked with stewarding building project funds, became Beacon Interfaith Housing Collaborative and is now the largest developer of supportive housing in the entire state of Minnesota.

When Christians enter the arena of affordable housing, they can quickly find themselves caught up in a complicated web of legal, fiscal, and moral challenges, many of which were birthed out of a sordid history of community injustice.

Against these odds, churches like Calvary Lutheran, Heart of the Rockies, and Caldwell Presbyterian enter battles for the right to build on their property—fights they don't always win—as they seek to faithfully address homelessness with the resources they have.

We'll look now at two groups that took those confrontations further: Beacon Interfaith Housing Collaborative and Firm Foundation Community Housing. In their efforts to build affordable housing in their respective spheres, they were subject to significant pushback from powers that functionally ensure housing remains scarce for those on the margins, but they continued to fight anyway . . . and win.

Power—who has it and who can leverage it—reverberates in these accounts. As we've explored, the misuse and hoarding of power is one of the ways gospel rescue missions have historically failed to love their neighbors in the way Christ does. Jim Gertmenian, who served as senior pastor of Plymouth during the Lydia development and the formation of Beacon, puts this in profound theological terms: "It's not rich people helping poor people. It's about people who have some power learning to use that power in a way to disperse it and to create a just society. We're not just helping the 'down and out,' which is such a demeaning way to understand the work. We are trying to envision God's justice being lived out in the world."

Yet the misuse of power is a feature, not a bug, of housing policy at every level of government. When Beacon and Firm Foundation began building housing, they found themselves in conflict with powerful people, institutions, and the ever-elusive yet omnipresent "way things are." Their stories feature confrontations and triumphs over the "powers that be" that make and keep people homeless. In their direct, nitty-gritty housing policy work, they help us get beyond just imagining a world where everyone has adequate housing—they clear the path and show us the way home.

* * *

"Housing development, if it's to serve people who are currently being underserved in a community, is always a policy issue."

Emily Goldthwaite currently serves as Beacon's director of congregational organizing—as unique a job title as I've ever seen, and equally essential. Her role is to engage and mobilize member congregations of Beacon's collaborative, of which there are now nearly seventy, toward sustaining and expanding their vision for everyone to have a home.

Before becoming Beacon Interfaith Housing Collaborative, they were simply a nonprofit extension of the Plymouth congregation. Even in these early stages, they learned quickly that NIMBY protests were only the first level of resistance they would encounter to any given project. Indeed, Carol Truesdell, who served on the early board of what became Beacon, recalls Lydia's successful launch as a crystallizing moment. They resolved then that such obstacles would not deter them from following their call to provide housing for those with the greatest need.

In technical terms, this meant they would be building housing for those at or below 30 percent of area median income (AMI). AMI is a tool municipalities use to assess income levels within a community. Developers always have a particular target market in mind for the housing they invest in and hope to get a return on.

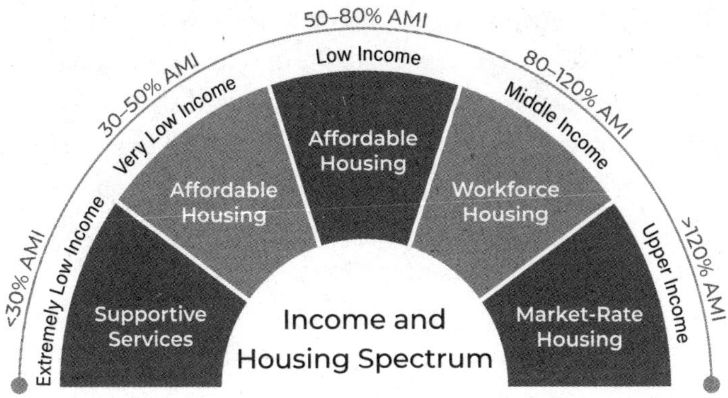

As an example, somewhat simplified for our purposes, let's imagine a city where the AMI for a household (perhaps a family of four) is $100,000 per year. To be at the 30 percent AMI mark or below—qualifying for Deeply Affordable housing—the household would be making below $30,000 a year. By this same metric, though, a developer could build their housing at the 50–80 percent AMI rate, still label it as "Affordable," and receive some of the benefits of doing so, even though the households being served are closer to AMI than they are to deep poverty.

If AMI is $100,000/year

AMI Level	Income	Housing Category
< 30%	< $30K	Deeply Affordable
30–50%	$30K–$50K	Affordable
50–80%	$50K–$80K	Affordable
80–120%	$80K–$120K	Workforce
> 120%	>$120K	Market Rate

A development's target market impacts the types of financing likely to be available to the developer. If a developer is building market-rate housing, they're unlikely to have any issue securing a loan, as lenders generally trust that the loan will be repaid through the collection of market-rate rents. But the more affordable the housing aims to be, the lower the yield on rents, and the harder it is to convince lenders that the loan will be paid back, making financing trickier. Developers like Beacon have to resort to stringing together funding from all levels of government, combining tax credits and bonds as well as seeking out private donations to cover the cost of building such units.

And that's just the cost to build. Operating and maintaining housing requires ongoing funding too. For this, Beacon depends on housing vouchers and other programs to make up the difference, placing the survival of their projects largely outside of their control. This is a key reason why affordable housing doesn't simply occur naturally in our economic system. Where housing is a commodity to be bought, sold, traded, and speculated on, the ultimate driver is profit maximization. Governmental attempts to incentivize truly affordable housing development through the above strategies are unable to compete with the sizable returns produced by market-rate housing.

In the chart above, you'll notice that what is considered "affordable housing" encompasses everything below 80 percent AMI. This means that a developer or politician can publicize an affordable housing initiative even if construction consists exclusively of units aimed at those making 80 percent AMI. Nonetheless, stakeholders can wave the banner of "affordable housing" and congratulate themselves for purporting to have addressed homelessness.

Because of the way AMI is calculated, producing these types of units may theoretically benefit a community because it adds to the housing stock and is limited in what it can charge for rent. But with nearly half of all households in America "cost-burdened" (spending more than 30 percent of their income) when it comes to rent, and with such a glut of housing owned by corporations that can afford to keep units empty in order to keep prices high, we cannot expect "trickle-down" housing economics to solve this problem. Realistically, unless housing is targeted at 30 percent AMI and lower, it will do little to resolve homelessness.

But when developers like Beacon set out to create such units, even once community resistance has been addressed and financing secured, further challenges remain. Zoning restrictions, building codes, parking requirements, and so many other policies restrict what can be built and create major cost barriers to development. While many of these regulations are purported to guarantee "quality of life," they tend to serve the interests of those who enjoy an income well above the median.

For example, 75 percent of residential land in American cities is zoned exclusively for single-family homes, ruling out the types of dense construction needed to match population growth. This is largely because those who already own their single-family home want to keep their neighborhood looking and "feeling" a particular way, regardless of what their neighbors may need. All of this is rooted in racial discrimination; a vast amount of housing policy was enacted, often explicitly, to exclude people of color from being able to live in these neighborhoods. While discrimination based on race is broadly illegal, it's not illegal to discriminate against those who are poor—in fact, it's incredibly common.

So in 2014 when Beacon decided to build a supportive housing project for 30 percent AMI individuals aged eighteen to twenty-four—a majority of them Black—in Edina of all places, there was substantial resistance. For nearly a century, the city of Edina, a first-ring suburb of Minneapolis, had been home to a racial covenant that stated, "No lot shall ever be sold, conveyed, leased or rented to any person other than of the white or Caucasian race, nor shall any lot ever be used or occupied by any person other than one of the white or Caucasian race." While racial covenants like these were deemed unenforceable by the Supreme Court in the 1940s, Edina maintained its racial makeup through terror, such that in the 1960s residents openly bragged that Edina had "not one negro and not one Jew."[1] Even today, when much of the city's history has been symbolically repudiated, the city remains 82.5 percent white compared to Minneapolis' 61.6 percent.

While the opposition to the youth housing project never explicitly named race as a factor, they did hold a commitment to maintaining Edina's socioeconomic makeup. Part of Beacon's strategy, therefore, was to not let racism go unspoken. They approached the project as one that would address *both* the housing and racial injustices of Edina—daring the opposition to explicitly state their discriminatory intent, or at least to publicly oppose something that would reverse historical discrimination.

What really put Beacon's efforts over the goal line, though, was that they had the support of churches *in Edina*. Predominantly white and wealthy churches led the charge to say, Yes, we want this in our backyard—we want the makeup of our neighborhoods to change.

Garnering the support of local congregations became pivotal to how Beacon approached every new project. Congregations that had supported their projects from a distance began to be more strategically involved. With each new construction, Beacon added more and more faith bodies collaborating to address the specific barriers a given project might encounter.

Lee Blons, the Plymouth Foundation's first non-church-member employee and Beacon's eventual executive director (until her retirement in 2023), leaned heavily into calling congregations into their advocacy work. While Lee and her team knew that their technical expertise was important, the true power was in congregations' collective public witness. "It was people of faith being willing to just say, 'I would welcome these people as my neighbors.' It's just so profoundly part of the Christian message." Lee would also emphasize that this message is not *distinctly* Christian. Even though Beacon emerged from a Christian congregation, the organization is proud that they are interfaith, finding common ground in the mission among Christian, Jewish, and Muslim congregations.

As Beacon has continued to expand, their organizing has become increasingly specialized. Emily joked in our interview that so much of their work would never fit on a protest sign and, even if it did, it wouldn't make sense to most people. One such example came when they tried to secure financing for Emerson Village in 2020. The city of Minneapolis maintains an Affordable Housing Trust Fund (AHTF), procured via particular taxes and dedicated to supporting affordable housing development. These funds are awarded annually based on applications received, which are scored on their feasibility and impact, and then selectively greenlit by the city council. Beacon applied for the funds and received one of the highest scores of all the applications but was still not selected for funding.

This isn't uncommon—affordable housing developers know well that these rounds of funding are highly competitive, and that first-time approvals aren't typical. It's understood that you often have to "wait your turn." But Beacon felt compelled to take a deeper look at what did get approved that year, and they were concerned by what they found.

The year Emerson Village was denied, only 18 percent of the approved units were for 30 percent AMI and lower. Even the AHTF was prioritizing units built at the mid to upper end of what could be considered "affordable." Emily and her colleagues convened a meeting of Beacon's board and a team pulled from five North and South Minneapolis congregations. Despite the swirl of approaching holidays and an age-old caution against "biting the hand that feeds," she recalls the tenor of the conversation: "We have to speak up about this, because the work that we're doing for one building is actually exposing this huge crack in the system that needs to be taken care of."

And so Beacon presented their findings to the city council and asked a simple question: "Are you good with this?" As it turned out, the answer was *no*. The council simply hadn't questioned the program's ability to produce the desired results. It wasn't out of malice or even intent that the higher AMI units had been approved, but expediency. The projects with higher AMIs had quicker and cheaper construction estimates, and so the city council believed it was simply doing the right thing by producing more units at a faster rate. When confronted with this reality, though, they elected to rewrite the mission of the AHTF to prioritize 30 percent AMI.

The following year, more than 40 percent of the approved projects were 30 percent AMI and lower. In 2024, it was 54 percent. Emerson Village finally opened in 2025.

These are the types of initiatives that don't make headlines but still result in real, observable impact. One of Beacon's current advocacy efforts focuses on operations costs for the affordable housing they specialize in. While that may not sound particularly invigorating, it takes a lot of funding to operate supportive services like case management, let alone more mundane things like facilities maintenance, front desk services, property management, and security to keep buildings up and residents protected. But lest Beacon be accused of playing it safe, they are also years into a campaign to create a state constitutional amendment that would guarantee housing vouchers to all households below 30 percent AMI—the first of its kind in the nation.

Beacon believes that their coalition, rooted in its ability to galvanize people across multiple faith traditions, can bring everyone in Minnesota *home*. Whatever barriers they encounter, be they as imposing as systemic racism or as unassuming as the approval percentage of true low-income projects, they believe in the power of people to organize and make change. Emily says it best: "It's shaping systems to be more just; to match our values."

* * *

When Taryn Sandulyak went for a routine prenatal checkup, her doctor gave her unexpected news. While it was presumably dressed in more professional-sounding language, Taryn remembers it in blunt terms: "You're going to have to calm down, or we're going to have to admit you and we're going to have to get your baby . . . you're a mess." Earlier that day, in her job with the city, she'd been tasked with evicting an unhoused woman from city property. For the better part of the past year, Taryn had tried to find somewhere this woman could go, but time had run out and she was called on to complete the eviction. For her and her baby's health—and so she would be able to sleep at night—Taryn knew she had to make a change. She took some time off, and then the COVID-19 pandemic struck.

During this same tumultuous season, her home church, Hayward Presbyterian, was years into a proposed housing development on their property: six tiny homes on five unused acres. Thanks to her familiarity with the city's project review process, she had played a key role on the committee. Even with the benefit of her expertise, the process to get the project approved took three long years. They opened to their first residents in February of 2020, around the same time as Taryn's health scare.

The final push for Taryn to make a change came from the University of California Berkeley's Terner Center for Housing Innovation. In May of 2020, they released a report titled "Mapping the Potential and Identifying the Barriers to Faith-Based Housing Development."[2] This survey identified more than twelve thousand acres of developable land owned by religious institutions across California's five largest counties, and it also demonstrated how this land could meet the affordable housing needs of those communities.

This report would have ripple effects across the entire state, and both an immediate and long-term impact on Taryn's trajectory. The report's release and Hayward Presbyterian's successful opening caught the attention of some other churches and Taryn, desperate for a new vocation, was ready to answer their call. She formed Firm Foundation Community Housing, and in their first year alone the organization built *seventy-four units.*

Taryn attributes this early success to converging pandemic realities: funding increased for public health resources for vulnerable populations; professionals with reduced work were motivated to do pro bono projects for the common good; the switch to virtual meetings enabled easier access to the movers and shakers capable of speeding up (or slowing down) development; zoning and land-use regulations were relaxed for projects aimed at mitigating the global COVID emergency.

When all of the unexpected benefits of pandemic development went away, Firm Foundation found themselves facing the same frustrations they'd experienced trying to open those first six homes at Hayward Presbyterian: long delays, rejections, exorbitant costs, and nonsensical laws. Just as Beacon's founders had, Taryn quickly became an expert in housing policy, especially in all the ways the rules worked against their mission to provide efficient yet dignified housing for people experiencing homelessness. She says, "We [at Firm Foundation] have identified the areas in which the system itself prevents housing from being built, and who says that *this* is the kind of housing that can be built, or is easy to be built, that the system *wants* to be built, but that is not meeting the need."

In the same year that Taryn created Firm Foundation and the new organization solidified its reputation and mission, the

Terner report was galvanizing other faith groups across the state of California. A self-proclaimed "Yes in God's Backyard" (YIGBY) movement coalesced as a counter to NIMBYism, advocating implementation of the Terner report's recommendations. Organizers with this group, familiar with the policy hurdles that churches willing to build housing often encounter, imagined a statewide bill that could streamline the process.

As the bill was in its developmental phase, one of its chief architects, Abram Diaz, met Taryn at a gathering to celebrate another bill that had been recently passed to streamline affordable housing. Abram touted the newly passed bill's potential, but Taryn was brutally honest that it would have little to no effect on her developments—that for her and other developers working on church land, it was essentially unusable. A couple weeks later, Abram called her to talk about the YIGBY group's hopes and invited her to join the work, to ensure that the bill would be written in a way that maximized its potential for developers like Firm Foundation. Taryn agreed.

This culminated in the formation of Senate Bill 4, known as SB4 or the "YIGBY bill." Senator Scott Weiner sponsored the bill, intended to create zoning and land-use exemptions for faith-based organizations to streamline the production of affordable housing on their property across the entire state of California. In support of this effort, the Terner Center released a follow-up report in August of 2023 that expanded their survey beyond the five largest counties and found 171,749 acres of potentially developable land.[3]

After numerous iterations, with Taryn submitting amendment after amendment to ensure a viable review and approval process, SB4 was voted on and signed into law in November of 2023. The first project approved under the new bill was one of Taryn's: five tiny homes at Bethel Community Presbyterian in San Leandro. The project had been in development purgatory for three years but, with SB4 in place, Firm Foundation submitted an application in February 2024 and it was approved by March. The success of SB4 has inspired cities and states across the country to pursue similar bills, which could be a complete game changer for affordable housing development across the nation.

Even with SB4, though, the advocacy work continues. A couple years in, Taryn has already identified weaknesses in the bill that could be remedied to make it even stronger. Getting a development approved is one crucial step, but many hurdles remain after. One issue is the cost of hooking smaller units up to utilities. A city or county typically connects plumbing to new developments, but at present no designation exists for tiny homes, even those intended for the formerly unhoused—just single-family or multi-family projects. On one current project, Taryn was quoted more than $400,000 to provide plumbing to just six tiny homes. These outdated and rigid rules, and the way that money moves through these entities, present ridiculous barriers that stifle important projects. Taryn is now working on a bill modeled after an existing one in Maine that allows projects to be approved all at once and at the state level, removing even more bureaucratic barriers that arise as different municipalities and levels of government get involved.

Firm Foundation, along with all the faith advocacy groups that helped develop, champion, and pass SB4, have laid a foundation for faith-based organizations to more easily participate in the movement to house our neighbors. Their detailed knowledge of structural barriers to deeply affordable housing can help guide us all into action: "For those of us who are privileged, it's our job to make the system work better for everybody," Taryn argues. "It's not enough to sit there and say you love your neighbor. It's not even enough to sit there and say we'll give you our extra land. Come fix it so that more people can do this."

* * *

If I had a dollar for every time someone asked me about tiny homes, I would probably have enough money to build a thousand of them.

Tiny homes have become a buzzword in discussions around addressing homelessness. With affordable housing so scarce, these efficient units play into our proclivity for scalable and innovative solutions. It's also something of a catch-all term, as these projects range from glorified sheds (without insulation, temperature control, plumbing, or electricity) to fully ADA-accessible homes with all the amenities of a permanent home, and the structural integrity to match. Hundreds of projects across the country fall somewhere along this spectrum.

When it comes to tiny homes—as with all else—we must remember that impact is more important than intent, and it's not only what we do but *how* we do it that reflects our values and contributes to outcomes. Popular discourse around tiny homes rarely goes beneath the surface of "Look at this great thing we're doing!" and "See how many we're able to build for so cheap!" Novelty and efficiency may be strategically prudent, but they are not values of the kingdom of God. I have read about and toured so many "tiny home" projects that have garnered the general public's acclaim yet are an insult to the people who will come to live in them—akin to patting ourselves on the back for offering expired food to the hungry.

Taryn and Firm Foundation, who have built 150 homes in Alameda County in just four years, have learned the hard way what it costs to choose dignity: "You're in this weird spot where if you do less, you can maybe build more for cheaper, but you have to lose so much in order to meet that threshold. And I'm not willing to do that." One of the sticking points for Taryn is bathrooms in each unit. Other tiny home developers talk themselves out of the need for individual bathrooms (rather than shared, exterior ones in a "village" setup), even though the people intended to live in the homes frequently have disabilities. Firm Foundation has counted the costs—literally—but remains stubborn that dignity and permanency are priceless.

This stubbornness confronts what I believe to be one of the most insidious powers operating in our world, especially when it comes to addressing social ills: complacency. Through a combination of ignorance and self-satisfaction, those without the experience of extreme poverty or homelessness are quick to compromise on services they've been lucky to never need. Phrases like "it's better than nothing" and "they should be grateful" and "beggars can't be choosers" emerge from this vantage. In this view, all the myths and arrangements that create and exacerbate homelessness remain uninterrogated. The hierarchy between those who serve and those being served remains in place as the egos of the powerful are elevated over the needs of the underprivileged. Needs essential to human flourishing are reduced to cold economic transaction.

For this reason, Taryn is a fan of small projects, like the one she opened right after we first spoke: six tiny homes designated for homeless seniors at Grace Presbyterian Church in Walnut Creek, California. Smaller projects allow for attention to detail and decisiveness about dignity. Tiny home villages that ambitiously aim for hundreds or even thousands of units tend to compromise in these areas and require vastly more investment and participation in order to be successful.

By contrast, these smaller projects keep buy-in and commitment manageable. Overstretched nonprofits, municipalities reluctant to make enormous investments, and churches taking a bold new step all have a greater chance at success. For churches especially, Taryn touts small projects between five and twelve units: "This is a community that [churches] can integrate. Churches that are doing small projects with so much intention and so much coverage, have the potential to do so much more benefit, both for the residents, but also for our community—acknowledging our connectedness."

* * *

In 2022, twenty years after Lydia Apartments' beleaguered opening, Beacon Interfaith had to reapply for the tax credits they had initially received for the building. Their commitment to keeping the units affordable was never in question. However, renovations were also due, and in the process of overhauling, they hoped to add a few more units. At the encouragement of someone from the neighborhood, though, they thought bigger.

They doubled the size of the building, from forty to eighty units . . . and no one protested. Save for a lone opposing comment about obstructed view, the community stood with

Beacon and championed Lydia's expansion. What the community had once derided as "a monster of an idea" was now a source of pride. As Emily believes, "It's not by accident, and I don't think that arc necessarily was going to bend toward justice if people hadn't intentionally done the work that it took to change the culture of accepting affordable housing anywhere in the city."

Confronting the powers that be, whether they take the form of individual ignorance, institutional policy, or systemic inflexibility, is not for the faint of heart. It requires dedication, organization, strategy, and a willingness to have hard conversations over and over again. And while it will almost certainly come with its fair share of difficulties and losses, victories are won: vulnerable people find home, laws change, and whole cities are transformed. As community activists chant: When we fight, we win!

Go and do likewise

Housing is a justice issue; and by extension, it's a gospel issue.

Churches across the country are stepping forward to leverage their land and financial resources to create housing and set it aside for those who need it most. A few groups, like Beacon and Firm Foundation, used the success of one project as a catapult to dozens more, making a meaningful dent in the extreme shortage of affordable housing in their areas. More than that, they confronted sociopolitical systems and successfully changed them in long-lasting ways.

In each case, this stemmed from a few core beliefs: (1) that developing housing is a call that churches should not only attempt but see through, even in the face of fierce resistance, and (2) that churches must engage politics for the sake of the marginalized. Over and against the insular and "nonpolitical" stance of many churches, and certainly most gospel rescue missions, these churches and organizations recognize that doing gospel work requires engaging and overcoming the forces that function to create and then target the "least of these."

Not every church must pioneer a nonprofit, develop hundreds of units of housing, and influence policy. The stories of Beacon and Firm Foundation are not about one person or organization taking on the system alone; their successes were possible because of coalition building and timely, local activation. When Beacon proposed a new project, it was the congregations, of multiple faiths, in the immediate area standing up and saying *yes* that moved the neighborhood past NIMBYism. Firm Foundation relies not only on churches who will welcome development onto their land, but the partnership of other churches to show up to land-use hearings and speak in support. SB4 was the result of decades of faith advocacy across California that culminated in a crucial moment to push a single piece of legislation over the finish line. We will need faithful leaders and innovators in this movement, but equally important are the tens of thousands of churches who stand ready to support the movement when the ground begins to shift.

When faithful people across the country organize around affordable housing in solidarity with our neighbors experiencing homelessness and housing insecurity, we can trust that God is on our side—and with all the power of the people, compelled by the gospel of good news to the poor, there's nothing we can't accomplish.

FIVE

Flexing Church Capacity, Expanding Church Community

Community House—Scottsdale, AZ

All Saints Episcopal—Portland, OR

Safe Parking LA—Los Angeles, CA

Bridge of Hope—National

Let's face it: not every church can sell, repurpose, or develop land for affordable housing. And while the proliferation of such housing is the best long-term investment for alleviating the problem of homelessness, there are hundreds of thousands of people living without homes *right now* who need and deserve support and services. While some parts of the church will answer the call to end homelessness via housing itself, we also require efforts that meet people in the midst of their homelessness with lifesaving and life-sustaining resources.

If you were to survey the unhoused people in your community about resources they utilize, you would likely hear the names of a number of churches. Often, churches are not considered part of the continuum of care because they receive no government funding. Yet it's exceedingly common for churches to serve as an anchor for many of a community's most basic needs. When I worked at a secular nonprofit in Hollywood, our participants' weekly routine included the Methodist church for clothing and snacks on Mondays; the Presbyterian church for lunch on Wednesdays and every other Sunday; and the Adventist church for showers and a gardening group on Tuesdays and Thursdays. While organizations like ours worked to provide housing and case management services, we were constantly directing our participants toward these churches to meet their most pressing day-to-day needs.

But as we've seen by analyzing the rescue mission model, it can be easy for churches to fall into a transactional or paternalistic mode when offering tangible resources. The churches and organizations we will meet here all see those experiencing homelessness as worthy of support and care not because of who they *could* be, but because of who they *are*. They extend themselves not as saviors, but as friends.

These ministries of mercy, focused primarily on basic needs, are the most common way churches interact with homelessness. They can be small but impactful operations. I encountered dozens that have found a way to utilize what they have—however little—to offer needed resources like food, respite, clothing, showers, and more, always with an eye toward the God-given dignity of the people they hope to serve. Of course, I can't include them all here, so let these select stories serve as a mere sampling of what is possible. If it's true that "the church is not a building, but a people," then any congregation is able to effect positive change regardless of the physical resources they do or do not possess.

* * *

In the late 2010s, a church campus in Scottsdale, Arizona was home to two thriving congregations. When staff member Jackie Parks suggested that they open their showers a couple times a week to people experiencing homelessness, she was simply trying to live out an ethos she believed with her whole heart: "A church should exist for the sake of the place that it is put." She had no idea she was setting the trajectory of her life and ministry for the next decade and beyond.

There are few resources for people experiencing homelessness in Scottsdale, especially during the heat of the day. In such a harsh desert climate, being caught outside can be deadly. In 2024, the region experienced record-shattering heat: 143 days above 100 degrees Fahrenheit, with seventy of those climbing above 110. In that year alone, the city reported over three hundred heat-related deaths among people experiencing homelessness, a direct consequence of a failure to intervene on behalf of vulnerable people under unlivable conditions.

The shower program began humbly enough, opening twice a week for three hours. It took a while to get traction, but relationships formed quickly. Jackie noticed that while a shower would take less than ten minutes, many lingered for the entire three hours; escaping the heat, of course, but also talking, sharing, communing. Jackie leaned into this development. Indeed, when training volunteers, she emphasized this relational aspect as a priority: "Yes, get people in and out of the showers, but at the end of the day, if people don't walk away feeling loved and seen and heard, then [we may as well] shut it down."

They had steady volunteer participation from a variety of churches, even through the early stages of the COVID-19 pandemic. Eventually, though, things reached a breaking point. The pastor no longer wanted to host the program, and even Jackie's most dedicated volunteers were burning out. That's when the city of Scottsdale approached with a proposal: they would fund the church not only to host showers, but to expand their services from three hours to eight on Mondays. Knowing they were already so much more than just a shower program, Jackie said yes, and opened Community House AZ as a nonprofit on the campus, separate from the church.

Scottsdale's investment in the day-relief center was robust. The city provided funding for the center's daily operations and supplied case managers from an existing agency. Community House further bolstered its services to include a meal, food pantry, haircuts, clothing closet, and workforce development. Tables are placed at the center of the church's sanctuary for attendees to eat, with open space along the walls to lie down and rest. As significant as the resources provided is the space in which the participants are safe to simply *be*. While cities across the country have heavily criminalized homelessness—such that merely existing in public is punishable by citations, fines, and even incarceration—day centers offer refuge with resources and relationships amidst a world of harsh weather and policing.

Jackie understands the emotional and psychological implications of this as well: "I can't ever imagine a life where I am unwanted everywhere I go. How dehumanizing and traumatizing that must be. It was really important to us that people got to experience being a human with dignity and worth—worthy of love—for as long of a day as possible." Despite the limitations imposed by COVID-19, Community House bustled throughout the pandemic. The two once-thriving churches, however, both shuttered. In a strange reversal, the church campus was now empty on Sundays but buzzing with activity on a weekday afternoon.

That was, until the presbytery that owned the campus came calling. They wanted an active church on the campus and asked Jackie, who was already in the process of pursuing ordination in the denomination, to serve as the pastor. It was a nonlinear path to get there, but the idea of Community House as not only a provider of refuge for the vulnerable but also a formal church was a synthesis of all her hopes. To yet another unexpected request that aligned with her values, Jackie said yes.

Nothing about Mondays changed, but Community House's previous identity as a day center became foundational to its new identity as a church. Jackie didn't want Community House to be a church that simply *had* a homeless ministry, but rather a church that understood its homelessness work to be as central as their Sunday worship. Of course, some people only attend one day, and others both, but Community House maintains that they are one community: "Church and worship happens on Sunday *and* Monday. It's the most authentic, beautiful expression of church that we've seen. . . . We're learning how to be one big community of belonging."

I had the opportunity to visit on a Monday and see this firsthand. I met Jim, who was directing folks to the various resources; he's also the greeter on Sunday mornings. I met Margaret running the clothing closet, who also handles projection and slides on Sundays. Cameron, who normally runs the sound booth on Sundays, grilled burgers and hot dogs. On a sweltering Memorial Day afternoon, I witnessed everything Jackie had told me about. Folks moved freely and comfortably through the church, hanging out, conversing, serving, and being served.

Finally I met Joe, a recent graduate of the workforce development group who had just obtained full-time work at a car wash down the street. He apologized to Jackie for the new job reducing his presence at Community House, which Jackie of course understood. He'd come by to share his testimony and report on his recent accomplishment with the workforce development group. Jackie told me that the group, though it does lead to job placements, also functions as a support group for those frustrated and discouraged by seeking and maintaining employment. It was a serendipitous example of exactly what a place like this can offer: resources obtained, yes, but amplified by the sharing and celebrating of those victories within a community.

Community House has some uncertain days ahead. The presbytery sold the campus to a megachurch with plans to renovate and no interest in continuing to host Community House. They have some time, but at any point they could be issued notice to leave within sixty days. Jackie seems unfazed; despite waning support, pandemic-related closures, and much more, what began as a tiny initiative to offer a few showers a week has become an indispensable part of

Scottsdale's homelessness response. It *must* continue, and so she believes that it will—this unpredictable, atypical gathering, worshiping, eating together, preaching, and offering rest, hospitality, service, and solidarity.

Or, as Jackie calls it: church.

* * *

A volunteer at the Saturday meal at All Saints Episcopal in Portland, Oregon once remarked that she felt the Spirit of God in the community room while people ate heaps of shepherd's pie, more than she had in all her years of church attendance. Lindsay Strannigan, who organizes much of All Saints' Saturday ministries and often cooks the meals, reflects on this often. The church's lead rector, Rev. Andria Skornik, jokes that the Holy Spirit shows up precisely because of Lindsay's famous cooking.

Forty years prior, a small group at All Saints decided to start serving a weekly meal on Saturdays for "the down and out." In the decades to come, this meal would function as a cornerstone of both the church's identity and the neighborhood's support system. When Andrea came on as the lead rector in 2018, she did so with a penchant for social justice and a soft spot for people experiencing homelessness. But rather than seek to single-handedly jump-start new ministries, she sees her primary pastoral gift as "not getting in the way." When folks in her congregation feel a sense of calling or mission, she aims to support and empower them to accomplish it, and then to pastorally encourage the church to come alongside and share in that work. Such was the case when a couple members came to her with a map, noting that the existing distribution of food banks in the city of Portland left a sizable gap in the area surrounding the church. This led to the opening of a food pantry on Saturdays alongside the meal.

Seeking a church without a solely insular focus, Lindsay found All Saints and jumped right in. A growing group of congregants believed their Saturday ministry could be expanded beyond the meal and now food pantry. In partnership with the church's thrift store, they opened a clothing closet where Saturday's guests could have access to clean, gently used clothing. What they began to notice, though, was that the guests who were unhoused needed to visit the clothing closet over and over. With no place to launder their clothes, and with severely limited access to showers and hygiene supplies, each new outfit was essentially single-use. In search of solutions, some of the members of the newly formed Social Justice Committee heard about a local shower and laundry truck and invited them to make Saturday at All Saints one of their stops, perfectly bridging this obvious resource gap.

The shower and laundry truck's first Saturday at All Saints was just weeks before the mass shutdowns caused by the COVID-19 pandemic. While so much of the world slowed down, All Saints—in particular their outward-focused ministries—ramped up. Folks in the church began sewing face masks. Lindsay acquired hand sanitizer in bulk from a local distillery and was bottling it in her house for distribution at the church. Nearly every square inch of the church building was full of food, clothing, or something that would be sent out the door each Saturday to their increasingly desperate unhoused neighbors. The weekly meal and the food pantry both shifted to a drive-through model. During this time, when the traditional conflation of "church" with "Sunday worship" was collapsing, All Saints redefined for themselves what it meant to be a church.

While they still offer the drive-through option, the volunteers and guests of All Saints' Saturday ministries were eager to get back to being together. The food served each week is a draw unto itself—multiple sources confirm the legendary status of Lindsay's cooking. But it's the sense of community and kinship that elevates the whole enterprise. Andria extols "the need for community and a place where someone thinks you're amazing and treats you that way through a three-course meal." When the church conducted a "customer satisfaction" survey among their Saturday guests, a consistent theme emerged: All Saints was their primary community. Even though few attended the church on Sundays, they knew All Saints was somewhere they belonged.

The neighborly awareness behind nearly fifty years of identifying and bridging resource gaps has resulted in All Saints creating a weekly one-stop-shop for people to get a meal, a bag of groceries, a shower, laundry, and a new set of clothes. But as delicious as it undoubtedly was, the Holy Spirit likely didn't show up for the shepherd's pie but for, as Andria describes it, the "sense of welcome, acceptance, and love for who you are *as* you are." The multigenerational, sociologically diverse community formed at All Saints embodies a world where nothing separates us from the love of God, nor from one another.

* * *

When we hear *unsheltered homelessness*, we probably picture tents, tarps, or curled-up figures laying beneath awnings or bridges. In Los Angeles, researchers set out to understand another, oft-overlooked portion of this group: those sleeping in vehicles. The sheer numbers are eye-popping, with more than fourteen thousand in Los Angeles County alone. Incorporating this data into the homeless count numbers, those living out of vehicles account for 40 percent of those considered unsheltered.[1]

Sleeping in a vehicle pales in comparison to sleeping in a home, but it still offers a greater level of safety than the streets or even many congregate shelters. Being able to safely sleep and store belongings behind locking doors—even car doors—is a luxury worth holding on to. Yet for so many, even this marginal haven is fleeting. Los Angeles is just one of many cities cracking down on overnight parking, further imperiling those who have resorted to vehicular homelessness. I've heard the story countless times: a few unpaid parking tickets lead to a boot. Unable to pay the now higher cost to remove the boot, the car is then towed—with all their belongings still inside. The price to retrieve it from the tow yard is even more unattainable. In a matter of weeks, people lose everything, with no path toward regaining it. As more and more people are driven out of their homes and into their vehicles, the places those vehicles would otherwise park are being legislated and policed out of existence.

To meet the needs of this specific population, service partners set about developing the "safe parking" model. Empty parking lots are designated for nighttime use, allowing people living in their car to park without fear of ticketing, towing, or break-ins. Security guards keep watch over the lot, limiting access to approved occupants only. The occupants are afforded a space to sleep soundly, with access to electrical outlets and bathrooms. In many cities, case managers are available to meet with the guests at the beginning of the evening to support a transition toward permanent, stable housing.

While many businesses have abundant overnight parking, churches are ideal hosts for safe parking programs: their lots are often well-maintained, conveniently located, and, most importantly, go underused through much of the week. They can offer volunteers to stand watch overnight or to provide dinner, and their buildings generally boast restrooms, a kitchen, and other necessary components. It's less of a stretch, in theory, for a church to imagine a missional use of their parking lot than it might be for a superstore, or even a government building.

Emily Kantrim cofounded Safe Parking LA, the first and only organization solely dedicated to vehicular dwelling. She oversaw more than two hundred parking spaces across several sites in Los Angeles County—many of them on congregational land. The organization handles referrals, case management, security, and all other logistics so that partner sites only need to provide access to the lot and to the bathroom facilities.

Emily's experience working with churches has been overwhelmingly positive. The first site to open was at St. Mary's Episcopal Church. During an initial visit, she keenly remembers walking down the church corridors with Glenn, a member of the vestry, who turned to her and said, "I see no reason why we couldn't start a safe parking program here tonight."

This spirit of willingness was a revelation to Emily, who in her previous homelessness work was used to government's risk-averse, red-tape approach. "Hearing people living their faith and not allowing their conversations to be led with fear was a balm for all the meetings I [typically] had." This first site at St. Mary's operated for several years before the lot's small size could no longer justify the staffing requirements. Even still, the church allowed Safe Parking LA to use their office space for another five years until they outgrew that too.

What Emily appreciated most about the churches hosting these sites were the congregations' relational approach to the partnership. She cited examples of a church's social justice group or moms group taking the initiative to cook meals or play board games in the evenings with the guests. Theological concepts of justice and service got a chance to live and breathe. Emily is proud of the way it allows such churches a "way in" to the broader issues of homelessness in their community.

Through something as simple as permitting the use of parking spaces and restrooms at a time when the building is otherwise empty, churches can meaningfully fill a huge need for a specific subset of the unhoused population. Safe parking is a proven and easily replicable model that most churches could begin operating with little effect on their existing ministries.[2] It's a model that can work as a foot in the door for churches to engage their unhoused neighbors, or as an additional resource to already existing compassionate ministries. Regardless, when communities of faith recognize all the ways they are blessed with resources and choose to use them as blessing for their neighbors, they prove true what Emily believes: "Churches are wired for this work."

* * *

Not every church has space to utilize, not even a parking lot; either because they don't own it, or don't have the will of the majority. So what is a church like this to do if they want to join the work of ending homelessness? In the mid-1980s, a women's Sunday school class at Sandy Hill Community Church in Coatesville, Pennsylvania struggled with that same question, and in responding to it they wound up building a model that others can utilize.

Nearby to Sandy Hill stood a YWCA women's shelter for homeless single mothers. When a few of the women began regularly attending Sandy Hill's women's Sunday school class, their stories convicted the church members, eliciting not just compassion but a drive to do something about it. Edith Yoder, who grew up at Sandy Hill, remembers a fateful Sunday when a woman from the Sunday School class stood up at the close of the sermon to announce that she believed God was calling them to support homeless mothers.

Neighboring churches and other community members were invited into the initiative, and a committee of about forty energized individuals began imagining what was possible. They considered a number of options, including buying a building, before learning of a rental-assistance model with a high success rate—particularly among families. In this model, rental assistance would be provided for six to twelve months, decreasing gradually relative to an increase in a household's income and independence. This efficient and empowering model matched their resources, but still lacked the personal touch they hoped for.

A few committee members turned their attention to an effective model in refugee resettlement, where families would be paired not only with professional case management, but also with average folks in the community to function as mentors, offering advice, home-cooked meals, connection, and access to resources. The committee surveyed some of these mentors to learn what worked and what didn't—more than anything, the mentors wished they had received more training and instruction ahead of time. By combining the efficiency of short-term rental assistance with the relationality of dual case management and peer mentoring, and after a few trial runs to refine the process, they settled on a model and a name: Bridge of Hope.

Churches were eager to participate in this model, where eight to ten "neighboring volunteers" would support an unhoused family alongside a Bridge of Hope case manager. This added element of community connection, uncommon amongst typical housing programs, is what Bridge of Hope considers the key to its success. Anne Dunnenburger, Bridge of Hope's director of outreach, notes that this bridges under-recognized gaps in people's day-to-day lives. A personal reference to an honest mechanic, a job opportunity, or a dependable babysitter can make a profound difference for someone struggling to achieve baseline stability. And in the long term, once a given family has stabilized and the rental assistance and case management are no longer necessary, the community remains, such that, as Anne remarks, "The next time they have a crisis, they're not coming back through the system again."

Over the course of more than thirty years, some things have of course evolved. Rental assistance now extends for up to two years, given the immense barriers to independence. Case management has become even more professionalized, ensuring that families receive high-quality services. And the program to train and prepare neighboring volunteers has grown into a robust, theologically and sociologically rich curriculum that educates on such essential topics as family homelessness, cultural humility, trauma-informed care, and the strengths-based approach. Edith Yoder, who was there at Sandy Hill at the start of it all, now serves as its CEO.

Bridge of Hope operates in twelve states, either as direct or licensed affiliates. Direct affiliates operate out of their national nonprofit, but others license the model, using their patented training curriculum and rental assistance protocol to operate independently. This has been an especially good fit for existing nonprofits or ministries who were serving families but lacked a model for addressing housing in particular. One such licensee is in fact a rescue mission; recognizing the opportunity to enhance its housing outcomes and focus, they turned to Bridge of Hope's proven model.

Edith is clear, though: while churches are their primary source for neighboring volunteers, Bridge of Hope is not an evangelistic ministry. "This is not an opportunity for proselytizing. Conversations might come up as part of a relationship, but it's a different starting ground." Edith noted in our conversation that part of what consistently confirms this approach is how often the families who come through the program already have faith. They don't need to find Jesus—they need housing!

In fact, many churches are seeing housing needs emerge from within their own congregations and are seeking out Bridge of Hope as a solution to serve their own. As the gulf widens between families' resources and the increasing cost of living, churches that have long been shielded from such realities are now confronted with the threat of homelessness amongst their members.

Whether responding to needs they perceive as internal or external, churches can find in Bridge of Hope a way to focus on neighborly support as a supplement to the work professionals do best. As an add-on to existing ministries, or as the passion project of a small group of dedicated individuals, Bridge of Hope brings a comprehensive and time-tested response to ending homelessness.

* * *

I was once invited to a virtual meeting hosted by Hennepin County, Minnesota, where I live, alongside a select group of homelessness service providers to give input on how to allocate a significant sum of new funds. The options regarding what to fund were plentiful: day centers, outreach, shelters, case management, meal services, administrative costs for nonprofits, homelessness prevention, housing vouchers, and constructing new housing. We discussed and debated where the gaps in our community were and what should be prioritized.

After going at this for a while, we began to zero in on a growing frustration that we were forced to choose between things that were all desperately needed. Do we invest in helping keep the person currently experiencing homelessness healthy and safe? Or should we prioritize keeping those on the brink of homelessness from ever falling in? Or should we invest it all in housing, knowing that this would carry the greatest long-term impact but the lowest in the short-term? The choice seemed impossible because what we really needed was enough resources to do all these things more, both robustly and quickly.

Every church can play an active role in the emergence of a world where everyone has a place to call home. Within that hope, though, there are churches whose limited size and resources preclude them from long-term, large-scale, capital-heavy investments, leading them instead to addressing immediate needs with people power. This is not a betrayal of best practices, but an essential aspect of it; while we are not called *only* to bandage wounds, bandages serve an irreplaceable function within emergency aid while waiting for comprehensive treatment.

Go and do likewise

Engaging these ministries, I was reminded of the maxim attributed to George Washington Carver: "Start where you are, with what you have. Make something of it and never be satisfied."

Each ministry began with what they had—a forty-year lunch service; a single shower; a parking lot; a small but dedicated Sunday school class—and offered it for the sake of their community. Beginning with one identified need, they continued to ask what more was required and then set about doing it. Instead of getting comfortable in whatever work they were already doing, they introduced more and more critical services to fill gaps identified by those they serve. Where the needs exceeded their expertise, they sought out professionals, leveraging their ability to provide space and volunteers in partnership with government resources already allocated to serve that population.

These ministries offer a glimpse of what the church could be: a gathering of unlikely people across traditional boundary lines of status, age, profession, and culture, participating in sacred community amidst the seemingly mundane acts of eating, sleeping, and showering. As Christian ethicist Laura Stivers writes, "Congregations might start through service but hopefully will take the next steps of making their worship service and church programs inclusive of all class levels, including the chronically homeless. . . . Bonds of solidarity can be formed and community life can be enriched in congregations with an orientation of radical inclusivity."[3]

In some cases, the relational aspects of the work are so enriching that they become the core driver of the mission. We turn now to two such examples that find and create joy through close reciprocal relationships with those on the margins.

SIX

Finding Joy in Smallness

Lazarus—Atlanta, GA and Washington, DC

Central City Community Outreach—Los Angeles, CA

When people hear about Lazarus, an Atlanta-based nonprofit, they would rightly assume that the name gets its inspiration from the Bible. But they usually guess the wrong story.

Executive director Johnny Winkle understands why. The story of Jesus raising Lazarus from the dead is certainly the most well known, and while Johnny doesn't like the exaggeration, nor the implied savior complex, that their nonprofit's work consists of "raising people from the dead," it's undeniable that it has elements of resurrection and new life.

Instead, Lazarus draws its name from the lesser-known parable of an extravagantly wealthy man and a sick and starving beggar—Lazarus—suffering at his gate (Luke 16:19–31). In Jesus' tale, both men die, but they wind up in very different destinations. The rich man finds himself tormented in hades, while Lazarus is carried to Abraham's side. This stunning reversal of social hierarchy always stood out to Allison McGill, who founded Lazarus while she was working as a personal assistant for professional athletes. She returns again and again to a central memory from the organization's early years, when she was doing Lazarus work in her spare time while still juggling her full-time career. One day she was tasked with returning a jacket a client had purchased, and she noticed the jacket cost more than Lazarus had recently spent putting on an entire Health Day event for unhoused people in Atlanta. This served as a stark reminder that there are rich men and there are those like Lazarus, and that she had more in common and connection with the latter.

Homelessness is a crisis as big as the vast discrepancy between available affordable housing and those that need it. But it is also as small as the relational distance between you and the unhoused person who camps in your neighborhood, sleeps at your bus station, or attends your ministry. Addressing homelessness is a delicate dance of striving for broad, systemic change while also being attentive, responsive, and in genuine reciprocal relationship with people in your immediate vicinity who experience homelessness and housing insecurity.

In the previous chapter, we focused on the tangible needs that churches met with their capacity, while also noticing how those ministries had an eye toward building community. The two organizations featured here are even more uniquely dedicated to the intangible ways that relationships lead to fostering joy and dignity. They exemplify faithfulness in small but eternally significant ways—knowing deeply that the most human and most *Christian* way to confront homelessness is through authentic and mutually enriching relationships with the unhoused. Unlike the story of Lazarus and the rich man, we need not wait until death for our social hierarchies to be inverted. We can instead practice a form of solidarity that flattens hierarchies and creates real community.

* * *

Allison McGill refers to the first year of her work as "the year of failure." It's a bit harsh, considering that the seeds of what makes Lazarus great were planted from day one. It all started on Thanksgiving Day 2000. Like many, Allison was moved to serve the unhoused with a group of friends that day, but she kept getting turned away. A week before Thanksgiving, Atlanta civil rights leader Hosea Williams had died. His legacy of feeding people—on Thanksgiving in particular, no less—and his untimely death inspired an unprecedented number of people to volunteer that day. Thousands poured out of their homes to lend a hand.

As Allison and her friends drove from place to place, they noticed a parking lot where a group of unhoused people were gathered, apparently not partaking in any of the numerous available meals. Allison and her friends decided to buy food from a nearby gas station and take it out to them. They wound up staying all day. "Something really impacted me that day, but it wasn't the food we gave out. It was the conversations we had. So we went back the next week, the next week, the next week," Allison recalls. "I was compelled to go back to the same place. I wanted to see how the couple of guys I had talked to were doing."

A month into this routine, the church Allison was attending decided this consistent outreach work should become a funded and supported ministry. In these early days, there was a lot of learning from mistakes. Allison would give out large sums of money or put people in hotels without an exit strategy. It's not that giving out money or putting people in hotels is bad, necessarily, but Allison recognizes that it came from a desire to *save* people while also misunderstanding her relative social location: "I was coming at this like: 'I have a car, home, and job, so listen to me.'"

Allison refers to the second year, during which Lazarus would get its name, as "the year of cleansing." She recounts learning to reject any sense of superiority over the people she encountered on the streets, and to repent where it crept in—a practice she continues to this day. In learning this lesson, Lazarus came to rely on a simple phrase—"with, not for"—that would define their work for the next twenty-plus years.

In practicing "with, not for," Lazarus began recognizing the value of fun as a core aspect of human dignity. Games and other activities were a fixture of their weekly outreach. The fun really ratcheted up when they began hosting a Super Bowl party. Recognizing that the simple lack of TV access meant that unhoused people couldn't participate in this annual cultural tradition, Lazarus stepped in. The event features photo booths, raffles, food, games, and, of course, watching the main event together—complete with characteristic cheering and jeering. While there is a service element to it in the form of setup, cleanup, and providing food, Allison likens it to hosting people in her home. "If you come over to my house for dinner, yes, I serve you, I cook, and then what happens? I don't go and start cleaning. I sit with you and share life with you."

This emphasis on fun extends even to their more service-forward annual event, Health Day. While the primary goal is to bring medical and mental health services directly to people in an accessible way, Lazarus can't help but make it a party. A DJ plays, and sometimes even the mascot for the Atlanta Hawks comes out. "We try to make it a fun party that happens to have some medical stuff going on," Allison said with a laugh. Then she reiterated that the intent behind everything Lazarus does is to host "a dignified experience worthy of our friends."

Lazarus grew to become its own independent faith-based nonprofit in 2008. While expansive in its relationships, credibility, and reach, Lazarus remains a relatively small organization. The majority of the people-power comes from consistent, dedicated volunteers who make up the outreach teams hitting the streets on Tuesdays, Thursdays, and Sundays to hold sacred, consistent spaces for community and kinship. Volunteers and partnerships also make the big events possible. In addition to the Super Bowl party and Health Day, Lazarus hosts a Christmas dinner and a Spring Party. Despite all of this, Johnny and Allison are the only staff members.

Even with just two staff members, Lazarus also has a chapter in Washington, DC. This wasn't a typical growth-expansion model—Lazarus DC materialized because Allison moved there. Lazarus Atlanta was left in Johnny's capable hands, and Allison did the same thing she did back in 2000 on the streets of Atlanta: find gaps in care, and step into them with authenticity and mutuality. Much of the work closely resembles that done in Atlanta. The Super Bowl party remains a central tradition, though in DC it's hosted at Central Union Mission—yes, a rescue mission!—as are many of Lazarus' other programs. Other aspects are unique to their new home. During her first year in the nation's capital, Allison encountered some plainly dressed trick-or-treaters whose families were unable to afford costumes. So began the DC location's annual Halloween costume drive.

Whether it's thrice-weekly outreach, parties, or a costume drive, it's all about dignity: the dignity of being treated as an equal partner in a conversation and, over time, a relationship; the dignity of having fun regardless of socioeconomic status or circumstance; the dignity of a parent helping their kid dress up with their friends. This dignity can only reveal itself when we truly see those who experience homelessness as people who also experience all of life as full, equal, beloved children of God.

Charity cannot get you to dignity; in fact, a charity mindset may convince you to notice only a person's misery and miss their entirety. And while feeling guilty may cause you to donate more, it will also reinforce the myth that people with great need are "not like us." The distance (both literal and sociological) from which we give will grow farther and farther, and deceive us into believing that, ultimately, we don't truly *belong* to one another. From this distance, we never truly hear or see our unhoused neighbors, believing that what we choose to offer them is more important than what they say they need. In so doing, we fail not only to effectively address their homelessness; we miss out on a chance at sacred community.

Knowing our unhoused neighbors is more than a responsibility; it's a gift. And those like Allison, Johnny, and their hundreds of volunteers have received that gift and keep coming back for more. "I wish more people knew that the majority of our friends on the street are delightful people," Allison said. "And my life is fuller and better because of knowing them."

The most effective tool I've ever seen for busting myths and biases around homelessness is, without a doubt, human connection. For as much time as I've spent writing and speaking about homelessness and those who experience it, I am confident the single most effective way to change your mind is not through reading a book or hearing a lecture, but by spending time in community and relationships with people who are unhoused. Before long, and with incredible consistency, preconceived notions about homelessness melt away in favor of the full, authentic, vulnerable persons in front of you. When we open ourselves up to a person, and they do so in turn for us, we see ourselves in one another rather than the lies that separate us. The image of God calls out to and recognizes itself, reminding us all of who we are and who we are all capable of being.

* * *

Most people I know, including many unhoused people, wouldn't want to be caught dead on Los Angeles' Skid Row after dark. But for over twenty-five years, if you found yourself on the corner of 6th and San Pedro on a Wednesday night, you might hear something surprising.

If on that night you ventured into Central City Church of the Nazarene, located in an unassuming storefront property in the heart of Skid Row, you'd see a packed house—two hundred–plus unhoused people—laughing, cheering, and singing along to a karaoke rendition of "Bohemian Rhapsody,"

"Jolene," or "Play that Funky Music." This ministry of Central City is by far their most popular and well-known program, and it all started with a shared vision to plant a church in Skid Row—among, and even despite, the rescue missions.

Sixth and San Pedro is also half a block from the entrance to Union Rescue Mission, one of the largest gospel rescue missions in the country and a powerful player in Los Angeles' homelessness landscape. Scott Chamberlain, a pastor at Los Angeles First Church of the Nazarene (which you may remember began on Skid Row before fleeing decades later to the suburbs), discerned a need for an actual church to serve Skid Row's community. While we most often think of Skid Row as the largest concentration of homeless encampments in the United States, it also used to include an additional ten thousand low-income individuals, including five hundred families, living in the old downtown hotels.

While the missions provided (and mandated) chapel and Bible study for its guests, Scott and his group recognized what Phineas Bresee had nearly a century prior—it wasn't *church.* While a person lived at a mission they might hear sermons and worship music, but they wouldn't experience all that a true church can offer. Scott recognized a need for spiritual care and consistent community rooted in something other than the rescue missions' transactional gospel. And so Central City Church of the Nazarene was formed, and Scott became its first pastor. He and his wife moved into the Hotel Alexandria, one of the poorest apartment buildings in Skid Row.

As their congregation grew, they knew they had more to offer the community, and so some services-oriented programming began under the banner of Central City Community Outreach. For more than a decade their biggest and most well-funded program was Say Yes, a tutoring program aimed at filling the educational gap for kids living in the hotels, shelters, and streets of Skid Row.

Around this time, Tony Stallworth found his way to Central City. Having spent several years unhoused in San Diego and Long Beach and freshly sober from alcohol and cocaine, Tony and his wife Lucy found joy in service at Central City's church and community outreach. But Tony also loved to have fun, and he found himself yearning for parts of his old life, especially the bar scene and the accompanying karaoke. Tony and Lucy loved to sing. Tony knew, though, that if he went back to karaoke, the rest would follow—so he pitched to Scott the idea of hosting karaoke at the church. They tried it out, and the first week around seventy-five people came. The event didn't lose any momentum until the COVID-19 pandemic almost fifteen years later.

The videos I've seen of karaoke night are as delightful, awkward, and *real* as you can imagine. Some sing boldly, others timidly; some perfect in key and rhythm, and others to a beat (or lyrics) only they can hear. But *everyone* sings to a supportive and eager audience. There truly is nothing like it. Over the decades, it's been written about by the *Daily Mail*, *Huffington Post*, *Vox*, and countless other publications. In 2012, the *Los Angeles Times* pop music critic Randall Roberts wrote about his regular attendance at Central City's karaoke night and professed, "At Skid Row karaoke, they are all songs of hope."[1]

Karaoke night is all about joy—every Wednesday from seven to ten in the evening, a glimpse of heaven breaks into a place that sometimes goes by the moniker "Hell's Half-Acre." Tony loves that it's a way for people to have fun in an environment that is both safe and, for him and many others, temptation-free. For Scott, it's an opportunity for the community to come together, celebrate, and let loose. "It's always the biggest, most imposing-looking guys who choose to sing the emotional ballads," he said with a smile. This has him convinced that whatever tough exterior any of us have built, on the inside we all long for connection and healing.

Over the years, Scott's focus shifted to the nonprofit Community Outreach arm of Central City as its board chair, and Tony became the church's pastor. When Skid Row began gentrifying in the mid-2000s, most of the families living in the hotels were forced out of Downtown and into South Central LA. Shortly after, with no more kids to tutor, the Say Yes program was shuttered and Central City leaned into street-based services. Skid Row changed, and so Central City changed alongside it.

These changes didn't come without a cost. The Say Yes program was well-supported by churches and foundations that didn't sustain their generosity to Central City when the programs shifted. Over time, slowly but surely, the funding and support for Central City's programs dwindled, even as the congregation thrived in attendance and vivacity. But the church couldn't bring in much support through tithing, and the space that Central City rented for the last ten years became more and more dilapidated and unkept by the landlord, even as he raised their rent. In the summer of 2024, with a landlord wanting to evict Central City, Tony's health issues increasing, and no new funding for a new facility, Central City decided to close its doors after thirty-six years of developing community and kinship in Skid Row LA.

* * *

I never got to go to karaoke night at Central City. By the time I heard about it, COVID-19 had necessitated a hiatus, and by the time it restarted I no longer lived in Los Angeles. But I once heard Thomas sing, and it changed how I thought about music forever.

Thomas was a daily participant at The Center in Hollywood—the drop-in service center where I began my career in the field of homelessness. He was in his late thirties, a lean dancer with tight locs and a fascination about the world. When he was at ease, there was a lightness about him that told you he could never hurt a soul. But the severe and nearly constant Tourette's he suffered from conveyed something else.

Against his will, Thomas constantly made sudden, unpredictable movements with his hands and upper body, lurching and lunging. He would make the kinds of sounds you might hear in a *Jurassic Park* movie. During these episodes his eyes would be wide and alert, and his whole body would tense. All of this, combined with folks' implicit bias toward seeing young Black men as more dangerous, made it so that one of the gentlest souls I knew scared the living daylights out of most of our participants and volunteers. It didn't help that he constantly wanted to attend our quietest groups—yoga, mindfulness, etc.—precisely because they calmed him. On a good day, we could spare a staff member to sit next to him in these groups and talk him through his bouts, which could be lessened if never fully quelled. Most days we had to ask him to step out so that everyone else could enjoy the group.

I periodically dropped by Hollywood Presbyterian Church for their Wednesday lunch, one of a few services they've been faithfully providing in the community for decades. One of my favorite things about their lunch is the piano player. A longtime church member shows up every week and plays soothing, upbeat music while people eat. Serving a good meal weekly to a hundred of Hollywood's most vulnerable is a hard feat on its own, but I always appreciated these extra touches to make it more special. Guests were welcome to request a song and even sing along. It wasn't quite the raucous karaoke of Central City, but it was still a good time. One week, Thomas walked up and, after a couple of tries to eke out the words, requested "Fly Me to the Moon" by Frank Sinatra. I prepared myself to hear Thomas struggle through the song, and to offer encouragement and support once he was done.

Instead, Thomas treated everyone to a flawless, stutter- and outburst-free rendition of the crooner's classic. His entire demeanor shifted; the tension in his muscles released and allowed his shoulders to drop slightly. His eyes softened so much that it felt like looking into a different, though familiar, face. It was like we were all in a dream sequence, seeing Thomas for the first time in his fullness. All of our jaws were on the floor such that when he finished, we had to collect ourselves and remember to applaud. He smiled big, then gradually morphed back into the Thomas we recognized.

Many studies are being conducted to better understand the way music affects our brain; anecdotally, though, things like what we witnessed with Thomas have been observed countless times. People with amnesia, dementia, and even Alzheimer's have demonstrated an ability to remember songs and melodies even when they can remember little else—and sometimes those memories can be a bridge to others. This is what makes me sob at the end of Pixar's *Coco*. It's what made me sing "Amazing Grace" to my grandmother as she lay in the coma from which she never awakened.

Music and singing are conduits to something spiritual and eternal that we don't fully understand. So when Central City held karaoke, it was so much more than providing a safe alternative activity; it was more than providing fun and joy. At the intersection of despair, hope, joy, and rage, Central City's invites all of us to embrace and express what makes us human, and in so doing reflect to one another what is divine.

* * *

Lazarus' website is WeAreLazarus.org. That may have been by necessity, with other, more basic iterations of possible domain names probably taken—but to founder Allison, this digital address has come to mean a great deal. At some point along the way, she recognized that the truest thing about Lazarus—about all of us—is that we're the same. We all celebrate, we all groan. We all, whether we are unhoused and desperate or wealthy and "successful," have a fundamental need for community and relationship; to be seen and known deeply in our humanity.

In the hierarchies we have built, though, this is less and less possible. All kinds of segregation, whether intentional or de facto, prevent this kind of kinship across boundary lines—especially those of socioeconomic status. In this hierarchy, mobility is constrained for those at the bottom and discouraged by those at the top. The powerful offer charity from above when what is needed is radical solidarity.

This is what the story of the rich man and Lazarus is about, after all—an act of God that baffles and overturns the hierarchy. The rich man spent a lifetime pursuing the most lavish life for himself, all the while missing out on God's best for our shared life. And today we hear this two-thousand-year-old story where the rich man is never even named. History so often forgets the poor and remembers the powerful, yet in Jesus' telling and the subsequent passing of the story, the rich man is unidentifiable.

But we know Lazarus. When the world is right, whether by the privileged moving in solidarity with the vulnerable or by the final upheaval of God, we are all Lazarus. When the world is made new, we will know each other by name and, all together, we'll sing songs of healing.

Go and do likewise

Mother Teresa is credited with the directive, "Do small things with great love." When it comes to addressing homelessness, we need Christians and churches that will take enormous swings to fill nationwide gaps in things like housing infrastructure, health care, and politics. But we also need small-church homeless ministries filled with folks who will be faithful and humble in the ways they care and serve. We can all practice the idea of "with, not for"; no matter the scale of our ministry, we can abandon saviorism and paternalism and embrace authentic relationships and community.

When relationships and community blossom, it's only natural that joy and celebration emerge as a felt need and an organic next step. This can take many forms. In addition to karaoke, sports watching, and holiday parties, I've witnessed birthday celebrations, dances, choirs, banquets, parties-just-for-the-sake-of-partying, and so many other joyful expressions of humanity. The joy doesn't always have to be separate or special, though—it can be baked into the everyday. It can look like serving a dessert along with the meal your church serves, as a reminder that the meal you're sharing isn't just about what your body needs to live but also what our souls need to thrive. It can look like decorating a space with beautiful art or living plants to remind people that not only is beauty something they deserve to see and feel around them, but that they are themselves beautiful.

Another unique aspect of Lazarus and Central City, uncommon among homelessness organizations both religious and secular, is their willingness to adapt. When families were forced out of Skid Row, Central City didn't try to shoehorn in the tutoring program or continue it for its own sake, nor did it abandon the neighborhood of Skid Row to chase after funding. When Allison moved to DC, she didn't charge in with a predetermined model for "what works" nor lean too heavily on Atlanta's model. In both cases, these organizations listened to the neighborhood and responded.

When you get to know people who experience homelessness and share not just in their misery but in their full life, amazing things happen. Lazarus and Central City show a glimpse of what heaven is like by shaming hell with their joy and dignity. These authentic relationships can lead us into great fun, and—if we let them—they can also get us into good trouble.

SEVEN

"Nothing About Us Without Us"

Open Table Nashville—Nashville, TN

Street Voices of Change—Minneapolis, MN

Love Beyond Walls—Atlanta, GA

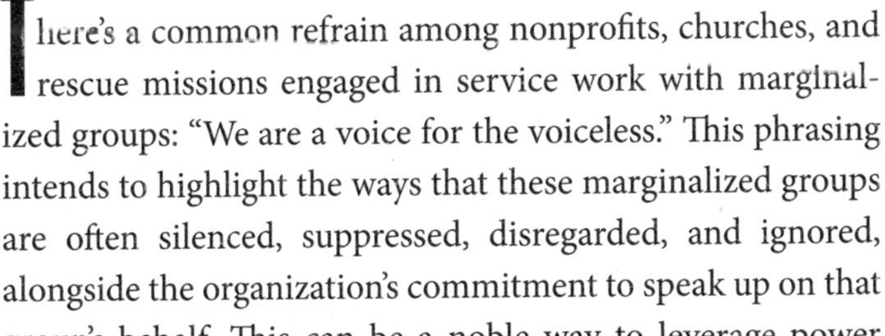

There's a common refrain among nonprofits, churches, and rescue missions engaged in service work with marginalized groups: "We are a voice for the voiceless." This phrasing intends to highlight the ways that these marginalized groups are often silenced, suppressed, disregarded, and ignored, alongside the organization's commitment to speak up on that group's behalf. This can be a noble way to leverage power and privilege to advocate for change; those whose voices are welcomed in spaces of influence can speak up for those who are not. Many powerful changes have happened this way.

But this kind of advocacy does not address the unjust power dynamic at the root of this fundamental marginalization. The people who already have power get to dictate what needs to change on behalf of those without power. And in translation, these demands can (intentionally or not) be filtered through the experience and preferences of their interpreter. Paul Boden, who founded two of the earliest and most influential homeless advocacy groups, writes, "You can't use charity as a substitute for change. You can't use bureaucracy as a substitute to fulfill a need, and you can't do things strictly for others. To be meaningful, change has to be owned and created by the people who are most affected or directly being hurt by what currently exists."[1]

Churches and organizations who aim to speak on behalf of the marginalized can, indeed *must*, go a step further, creating spaces and occasions where those with power and influence hear directly from those experiencing the fallout of their actions and inactions. The three organizations featured here all exemplify a commitment not just to utilize their power, but to share it. Much like the organizations covered in chapter 4, they go beyond models of charity, pursuing justice by confronting the powers that ultimately create and perpetuate homelessness. Where Beacon and Firm Foundation are focused on housing policy, these three concern themselves with the experience of homelessness itself, and with the powers that impose upon, punish, and mistreat people without homes. These organizations elevate and empower those who know firsthand how devastating—even deadly—our mismanagement of this crisis can be.

Dietrich Bonhoeffer famously wrote, "We are not to simply bandage the wounds of victims beneath the wheels of injustice, we are to drive a spoke into the wheel itself."[2] The groups we're about to meet heed this call, while also ensuring the work of stopping the wheel is led not by would-be heroes, but instead take its cues from those beneath the wheel in order to stop its crushing momentum.

* * *

Lindsey Krinks, director of advocacy and cofounder of Open Table Nashville (OTN), has been a Christian for as long as she could remember. Yet it was when she began working with people experiencing homelessness that she experienced another kind of salvation. "I was being saved—from myself and from a wayward society that told me my worth was bound up in what I accomplished, accumulated, and possessed."[3]

Years before the formation of OTN, Lindsey was deep in the dual work of outreach and advocacy. With a small group of like-minded people she had begun to go into encampments, in particular, a large, long-standing one called "Old Tent City." They would bring supplies and resources, and then also develop friendships with the residents. Very quickly they saw that this community faced serious unjust pressure from political forces, and that true support and friendship would have to include solidarity in the form of resistance. This aligned with a framework Lindsey was learning from the since-shuttered Power Project, a community organizing group led by people who had experienced homelessness. She explains,

> I was the learner—not the rescuer. They were teaching me that I could not ultimately address homelessness and

> other injustices through charity, service, and volunteerism alone. It would have to involve addressing what was upstream.[4]

By the time Lindsey cofounded Open Table Nashville in 2010 to continue this work, it was embedded in the organization's ethos that ending homelessness began with trusting, mutual relationships that then compelled them into just action in solidarity. Rather than speaking on behalf of the unhoused, OTN empowers their unhoused neighbors to speak for themselves, providing training on advocacy, media relations, and community organizing. When media asks for interviews, Lindsey and OTN step back, and the unhoused step forward. Several OTN staff and board members have experienced homelessness. Those experiencing the harm, they believe, are the ones with the solutions. And the most pronounced harm facing Nashville's unhoused is criminalization.

The criminalization of poverty and homelessness is nothing new, of course. It's part of what inspired Jerry McAuley to found the first gospel rescue mission and give the poor and unhoused a safe place to eat and congregate—much to the chagrin of local law enforcement. In his autobiography, McAuley recounts the cruelty and brutality of the police assigned to the poor area where he opened his mission, who would dole out regular beatings for mild and even falsified offenses. One particular officer would regularly storm into the Mission during their services and stomp on their Bibles.[5] The officer didn't hate religion—he simply despised the idea that the poor were worthy of care.

Over a century later, however, CityGate and its missions were far more comfortable with policing homelessness. When asked about criminalization in an interview with *Christianity Today* in 2021, CEO John Ashmen replied,

> What's missing here is a sense of responsibility. Because of our desire to be humane, we have taken away any sense of responsibility from people who are on the street. Yes, there's mental illness and there are addictions that have to be treated, but if you don't have a sense of responsibility and you don't feel some sort of pain from living this lifestyle, then we're going to see more and more people there.[6]

Open Table Nashville embodies a different way to faithfully engage homelessness. Tennessee, though, is a difficult place to do such work, and Lindsey and her compatriots have had their hands full just trying to keep a few of the city's biggest encampments safe from displacement and criminalization. They never could have anticipated how criminalization would sweep the nation and find its way back to Tennessee in a big way.

In 2018, tech billionaire Joe Lonsdale founded the Cicero Institute, a political think tank and lobbying group focused on the issue of homelessness. Their proposed solutions include abandoning Housing First strategies in favor of camping bans (along with $5,000 fines for violations), and the construction of new private prisons to incarcerate those who commit "public lawlessness." Lonsdale bankrolled anti-camping legislation in Austin, Texas, and Cicero has helped produce legislation in at least fifteen other states, with eight bills passing.

Criminalizing homelessness most often takes the form of "sweeps," referring to the closure of encampments by force.

Police and sanitation will arrive at an encampment and mandate that people vacate the premises within a short window of time. Anything not claimed immediately is trashed—everything from survival supplies to personal effects. If an unhoused person is away from their belongings during one of these sweeps (perhaps at work, or pursuing case management to end their homelessness), they stand to lose everything.

These sweeps are of course personally costly to those they target, but they are also exorbitantly expensive. In Minneapolis, it was calculated that every encampment sweep costs the city upwards of $120,000, and in three years the city spent $5.5–7.5 million closing camps.[7] Another study showed that it costs just over $30,000 per year to criminalize one person experiencing homelessness, when housing them would cost just over $10,000.[8] Pursuing the Cicero Institute's initiatives is, amazingly, far more expensive than the Housing First approach they lambast, and it produces no meaningful results—encampment closures only cause unhoused people to relocate, either to a new outdoor space or to jail, while causing untold harm to their progress, stability, and health.[9]

In addition to being more costly than housing and supportive services, sweeps fail to make communities any safer or more appealing for anyone. The unhoused are pushed into more vulnerable and isolated living conditions, deteriorating their health and increasing their desperation. To prevent encampments from reforming, authorities will place unsightly fencing, jagged surfaces, or even chunks of broken concrete in the spaces they "reclaim." Sweeps create the very realities they purport to solve—making our communities less safe, healthy, and desirable.

As Cicero has infiltrated legislatures across the country, they have secured big wins for their agenda at the expense of those experiencing homelessness and those who care for them. Arguably their largest victory was in 2022, when Tennessee became the first state to make sleeping on public land a felony based on the template legislation Cicero produced. For Open Table, this was a turning point. Forced to reckon with the ways their advocacy efforts had come up short, they recognized their focus on the larger cities of Nashville, Knoxville, and Memphis had neglected much of the state's political terrain, especially prominent rural areas holding significant political sway.

To counter this growing movement, OTN has adopted a new, more proactive posture. They continue to focus on coalition building but no longer wait until something destructive is happening to activate. Instead they aim to build power and infrastructure that can last. In 2025, they announced the formation of Housing for All Tennessee, a statewide coalition of five nonprofits across the state fighting for tenants' rights, housing justice, empowerment, and ending homelessness. One of their first actions together was at the state capitol, meeting with over fifty lawmakers to express support or opposition to multiple pieces of legislation related to housing and homelessness. More than half of the day's advocates had personal experience with homelessness or housing instability.

As they look toward the future, Open Table Nashville intends to continue their local and statewide efforts and perhaps expand into national organizing work—all while maintaining their on-the-ground outreach efforts. Executive director Allie Wallace affirms, "We want to meet your basic needs. But also we want to go upstream and figure out why you're in this encampment in the first place so that you don't have to be here again." And by advocating *with* people experiencing homelessness rather than *for* them—what Lindsey calls "passing the mic"—they ensure that the voices of those affected by the ways we cause, perpetuate, and punish homelessness won't just be represented; they'll be amplified.

* * *

In order to attend a meeting of Street Voices of Change (SVOC), I had to be formally invited. The meetings are only open to those who have lived experience of homelessness; everyone else is subject to a vote before they can attend. I went before their leadership team to make a formal request, where they asked me thoughtful questions about who I was and what my intentions were. After they took my request to the larger group for a vote, I was welcome to attend a meeting and observe.

At the meeting, which takes place weekly at Central Lutheran in Minneapolis (with another weekly meeting at the Basilica of St. Mary just down the street), I found a seat near Melissa Pohlman, Central Lutheran's pastor of community engagement, and Katie Dillon, the director of Align Minneapolis, a coalition of nineteen interfaith congregations committed to ending homelessness. I expected one or both of them to lead the meeting and do most of the talking—but I couldn't have been more wrong. Instead, the festivities were opened and facilitated by members of the group. In keeping with the prominently displayed rules of decorum, attendees shared updates on their current initiatives, heard from county representatives on data they had requested, and elected who would sit with me for an interview—all while eating breakfast. Katie and Melissa passed out papers and counted votes, functioning as assistants in the context of the meeting.

After a decade at Central Lutheran, Melissa was used to embracing the opinions of others, even when they went against her own instincts. When she first arrived at the church, she was tasked with continuing their ministries to the poor and unhoused, which had operated for fifty years. One of those ministries included a Monday worship service followed by lunch. Attending the worship service was not required to eat lunch, and many folks would only come for the latter. But Melissa, familiar with manipulative models that require folks to "sing for their supper," worried that even their proximity was problematic. She anxiously surveyed folks for months until one regular finally said, "Stop asking that [expletive] question! We came to a church expecting you to be a church." Her anxiety released, and from that point on she leaned in, building a monthly worship calendar based on what attendees said they hoped for from a church experience.

This commitment to hearing and responding to their guests came in handy when Align was in a refocusing phase. Surveying their regulars at the various congregations' ministries, Align heard over and over that folks missed a nonprofit's lived-experience advocacy group that had been short-lived. Melissa set about starting another such group, initially called Homeless Advocacy Network before renaming themselves Street Voices of Change (SVOC).

When Tyra was unhoused, her time in shelters was the most harrowing and dehumanizing aspect of her experience. She spoke with so many others who shared this indignation—mistreatment by staff, insufficient resources, safety concerns, or being kicked out unfairly—but no one felt they had the power to do anything about it. They were—justifiably—afraid that they could get kicked out for speaking up. As SVOC formed, this topic became the first galvanizing project. Working and sharing together, Tyra and the rest of the group began to believe they could do something about their treatment in shelters.

The group aspired to improve conditions at every shelter, but one in particular kept coming up: the local Salvation Army. As the largest shelter in the city, nearly everyone experiencing homelessness had passed through it at some point, or knew someone who had, and these collective experiences had given it a notorious reputation. By focusing their efforts and leveraging the power that Align held in representing so many church communities, the group managed to get the local Commander of the Salvation Army to attend a meeting and hear their stories. Melissa recalls that the Commander seemed horrified and did her best to truly listen. While no immediate changes resulted—the Commander took another position out of state shortly after—SVOC's confidence grew. They had managed to bring someone with the power to change their reality to *their* space on *their* terms, and they had been heard. They were building power and momentum.

With a few months of consistent work, they produced the Shelter Residents' Bill of Rights, containing ten reasonable expectations for how shelters should operate and how occupants should be treated. It includes standards for quality amenities and services as well as a grievance procedure involving independent representatives to prevent unjust exits or targeting. It was a hard-fought process to incorporate and distill all the negative experiences into a list of demands, but the final version is an impressively succinct yet thorough document.[10]

Now came the question: What to do with it? Who would willingly subject themselves to these tenets? Who would wield the power to enforce them? SVOC learned that Hennepin County was the governing body funding shelters, and therefore set the standards—and at the time, standards were incredibly low. And so conversations began with county officials, who were surprisingly receptive. As a result, the Shelter Residents' Bill of Rights is now included in every shelter contract administered by Hennepin County. Ever since, Hennepin County has had a standing invite to SVOC meetings, and representatives attend consistently.

The group is more than the sum of their victories, though there have been many. In addition to the Bill of Rights, SVOC authored an initiative to provide storage for unhoused people in a parking garage downtown, held candidate forums for city council and mayoral candidates, and addressed specific grievances at local nonprofits. Observing the group interact and speaking to some of their members, what I saw most prominently was a sense of pride and gratitude. Anthony[11] and Randip both admitted that the breakfast served at the group was a big part of the initial draw for them, but they also remarked that even participating minimally gave them a sense that they were part of something. Randip said proudly, "They at least give a voice to people that don't get a voice ever, and they get to get heard. . . . We've got a lot of grievances out there on the street. There's a lot that society has just decided not to see."

For Tonia, who has been part of the group for a few years now, it's also about the ways it transforms her negative experience into something meaningful for the community. "I believe that all my homelessness can only help somebody, 'cause we all walk homeless in a different light and if we just listen to each other, we can help each other." Where homelessness could breed isolation or even competition over minimal resources, SVOC brings people together over shared experience.

Tonia shared her initial surprise when she first came across SVOC: "I didn't know they had meetings for stuff like this!" At the time, what SVOC represented was uncommon; but, in part because of the success of groups like this, initiatives among homelessness services providers have increasingly incorporated those with lived experience in staffing and decision-making. Nationwide groups like the National Alliance to End Homelessness have made hiring people with lived experience a priority, as well as advocating for nonprofits and government entities to follow their lead. Because of groups like SVOC, "meetings for stuff like this" are happening more and more across the country.

It's especially significant, though, that advocacy that centers the marginalized happens in a church. Each of the members I interviewed had different relationships with faith and church, but all of them felt safe at Central Lutheran. By hosting and supporting (though not directing) SVOC, Central Lutheran and the other congregations of Align share power, undoing prevailing narratives that unhoused people are helpless or defined by their victimization. This dynamic enacts Jesus' most outrageous teachings, overturning our expectations about who has power in God's eyes—to whom the kingdom belongs, and who is first or last. Katie appreciates that in her work organizing Align's nineteen partner congregations, of different denominations and even faiths, she sees these disparate groups nonetheless come together on what matters most. "There are very few things that everybody in that room can agree on, but there is no question that every person deserves to have a safe and dignified home."

These days, SVOC is pursuing several initiatives all at once. They hope to enact the Shelter Residents' Bill of Rights at the state level; they're working on a public bathrooms initiative with the city council; they're enquiring with the county about the success rate of folks who are housed via programs; they're providing insight to local plans for safe parking and safe camping sites. Each of these initiatives either emerged from the group or was brought to the group by those with authority to seek their unique insight *before* moving forward.

Melissa reflects, "Street Voices is the ultimate result of turning towards folks who have lived experience and saying, 'What do you want? What do you need? What's going to be helpful to you? What do you want to see out of this?' And then get out of the way and let them do it. And find out what support they need to make it happen." This group is proof that not only are unhoused people the experts of their own experience, but also, if given the opportunity to become so, are the agents of their own empowerment and systems transformation.

* * *

On January 16, 2025, in the Sweet Auburn neighborhood of Atlanta, Georgia, an all-too-common sweep was demolishing an encampment. As city vehicles tore through the few belongings and makeshift homes of the unhoused residents, an officer was flagged down by Cornelius Taylor from within a crushed tent. Within a few minutes, Cornelius was dead. In the official police report, they claimed that his death was likely the result of an overdose, citing "no obvious signs of physical hurt." But the autopsy confirmed what everyone on the scene already knew: Cornelius Taylor died from blunt force trauma to his abdomen and pelvis, sustained when the front loader collided with the tent he was occupying.

Reflecting on this horrifying event, author, community activist, and scholar Terence Lester wrote of Cornelius,

> His life not only reminds us of how public policy and public sanitation sweeps target those who are unhoused but also how dehumanizing it is to have not only your belongings but even your existence swept away. . . . Sweeps disrupt lives, destroy communities, and send a harmful message to society that the lives of those who are unhoused are not worth it—they humiliate and harm rather than humanize.[12]

Lester rightly notes the way that sweeps not only cause an immediate detriment, but also stem from and contribute to harmful views about those who experience homelessness. "If society labels someone as lazy or dangerous," Terence points out, "then the policies built around them are going to reflect that assumption. They will be punitive, not restorative."[13] The perception that homelessness, and whatever results from it, reflect an individual failure is ubiquitous—whether performed by politicians, parroted by police "just following orders," or preached by gospel rescue missions. This stereotype is then regurgitated by media who neglect to look deeper and confront these authority figures with data and competing narratives. This vicious cycle leads to more sweeps, and more sweeps make homelessness worse, justifying even harsher approaches.

The need for advocates to confront these narratives is therefore incredibly important. This is the work of narrative justice, something that has invigorated Terence for more than a decade. He defined it to me it as "the intentional work of disrupting dominant stories that harm marginalized communities. . . . Narrative justice asks, Who controls the narrative? Who benefits from it? And who is erased by it?"

Lester and his wife, Cecilia, founded Love Beyond Walls, an organization with several initiatives that reckon with Terence's own intimate experiences with homelessness. Having once experienced homelessness in his mid-teens—sleeping in cars and staying with friends—Terence never forgot the sting of invisibility. Years later, when preparing to launch a nonprofit, he made the intentional choice to live on the streets again for several days, guided by the wisdom and invitation of his unhoused friends. Terence's journey—from being a high school dropout to earning a PhD—shapes every part of his advocacy. He knows what it's like to be counted out and unseen, and he's made it his mission to center the voices of those pushed to the margins.

In fact, Terence doesn't see meeting basic needs and narrative justice as separate. Reflecting on the earliest days of Love Beyond Walls' work, which was focused on providing handwashing stations and showers, Terence noted, "A need for a shower wasn't just about cleanliness. It was about acknowledgement. It was about being included in the basic human right to public sanitation. Public sanitation, for the unhoused, isn't just about health—it's about dignity." In this framework, every shower and every handwash confronts these narratives implicitly, even before vocal advocacy work takes place. Dignity is affirmed even before it is declared.

The theme of *dignity* emerges over and over again in Lester's writing and in the initiatives of his nonprofit. While Love Beyond Walls is not structured as a religious organization, its heart beats with the values of Terence's personal faith—especially the way Jesus practiced radical compassion, moved toward the margins, and restored dignity. As a faith leader, Terence is compelled by the example of Jesus, who consistently showed up for the most overlooked—washing feet, breaking bread with the outcast, and confronting systems that harmed the vulnerable. His work is not just social or charitable; it's spiritual. It's an act of discipleship rooted in proximity, presence, and a refusal to look away. The two most public-engaging projects of Love Beyond Walls are aptly named: the Imagine Dignity podcast and the Dignity Museum.

Imagine Dignity is intentionally raw and unfiltered—often recorded on sidewalks, street corners, under bridges, or near abandoned stores. Background noise, vulnerable pauses, and city sounds draw the listener into a sacred space where real people share real stories. Terence listens with deep presence, affirming dignity not just through words, but through witness.

The most innovative project of Love Beyond Walls is the Dignity Museum. Housed in a shipping container—itself a reminder that something transient can contain a multitude of narratives—the museum features stories, data, and pictures, as well as an engaging audiovisual experience using virtual reality to offer visitors an intimate look into the experience of homelessness. Because it is mobile, the museum has traveled across the state of Georgia and beyond.

When I asked Terence how he's seen the museum impact people, he responded,

> I've seen high school students cry after realizing their classmates were quietly experiencing homelessness. I've watched people who are unhoused walk through the museum and see their lives reflected with beauty and complexity. I've seen donors, educators, and community leaders leave the space changed. It's not just about learning—it's about recognition. Recognition is sacred. It's the beginning of restoration. The Dignity Museum doesn't offer artifacts. It offers humanity.

Humanity—the idea that each person is imbued by their Creator with inherent worth, purpose, and dignity—is rarely front and center when we talk about homelessness, and even less when we legislate around it. It was certainly not on the minds of those who ordered the encampment clearing that killed Cornelius Taylor, nor any other sweep before or since. We have opportunities, though—inspired by Lester, Love Beyond Walls, and everyone who experiences homelessness and dares to make themselves known—to tell a different story.

* * *

It's not just gospel rescue missions that face the temptation to override the wants and self-identified needs of the marginalized people they serve. Even the most well-meaning nonprofits (both faith-based and secular) and government entities, who may criticize other organizations for seeing unhoused folks as lazy or evil, can still enact their own form of paternalism by seeing the same folks as helpless or naive. Unhoused people are full of the same dreams and desires and instincts and flaws that we all share. More than that, their experience of homelessness has given them survival skills, resilience, and tested hope that those of us who have lived within society's tightly drawn boundaries could hardly imagine. In the same way that the organizations in the previous chapter embody a "with, not for" approach to helping work, Open Table, Street Voices of Change, and Love Beyond Walls enact "power with, not power over" in how they advocate for change.

As Christians, we are called to emulate that same characteristic that Christ embodied. As Philippians 2 charges us,

> Let the same mind be in you that was in Christ Jesus, who, though he was in the form of God, did not regard equality with God as something to be exploited, but emptied himself, taking the form of a slave, being born in human likeness. And being found in human form, he humbled himself and became obedient to the point of death—even death on a cross.

If Jesus could let go of power so as to share life (and death) with us, then those of us who follow him can aspire to the same; letting go of our need to control, manage, and *rescue* people, even in our well-intentioned efforts to change the systems that harm them. If we truly see Jesus in the face of the poor and unhoused, we ought to listen and be led by the truth they offer us.

By allowing folks experiencing homelessness to lead us where they want to go, we not only experience the gifts of solidarity with the unhoused, but we may actually see change that benefits all of us as a community fully realized. This will only happen if those of us with power and privilege leverage our resources and influence to support the leadership of those most affected, amplifying their voices and multiplying their power.

As Lindsey Krinks reminds us, "We are not a voice for the voiceless, we are a megaphone."

Go and do likewise

One of the things gospel rescue missions do well is to hire from within. Very often frontline staff are former program participants, which not only creates a sense of what's possible for those at their lowest point, but also ensures that those working closest with vulnerable people know what it's like to be in their shoes. It's not a perfect recipe for preventing abuse and harm, though, as the inherent paternalism of their model can create power dynamics even still. Those who are now out of that experience can wonder, "Why can't you just do what I did?" Additionally, it's rare to see these folks with lived experience allowed to rise above the lowest paid positions.

The difference, ultimately, is about posture: Do you consider a person's experience valid only if they've listened to and graduated from your program's tutelage? Or do you believe that the folks you serve are the experts of their own experience, and that the services you provide ought to meet their expressed needs? Do you have the humility to adjust if that fails to be the case? For the people and programs highlighted here, this posture led to a decision to create a space and opportunity for the voices and power of unhoused people to be cultivated, and then materially empowered to act in the community—to create change, to influence policy, to rewrite narratives.

While it may mean an adjustment in attitudes and perceptions, it costs little to add something like this to an existing ministry. For those churches who offer shelter, a food pantry, showers, or any tangible resource, you have ample opportunity to solicit the feedback of your clientele on your ministry, and of their broader experience. Surveys, listening sessions, and focus groups are great ways to gather and hear directly from those you serve, assuming you can create an environment of trust and transparency. This atmosphere is fostered or sabotaged in the smallest of ways—the language you use to create boundaries, the attitudes of volunteers, and how you handle the slightest setback.

If all you have at the moment is a group of people, housed and unhoused, willing to work together and value each other's resources and insight, you have everything you need to begin to make change. This posture of sharing and building power can pair easily with even the most basic of ministries to elevate them beyond mere compassion and toward a holy inversion of whose voices—and lives—are valued.

EIGHT

Nurturing a Mutual Spirituality

The Lamb Center—Fairfax, VA

FedUp Ministries—Washtenaw County, MI

Church at the Park—Salem, OR

In the fall of 2022, *Sojourners* published an article of mine titled "Too Many Christians Are Fighting Homelessness the Wrong Way," my first foray into analyzing gospel rescue missions and their model. I received a lot of responses from the piece, including many from rescue missions that disagreed with my conclusions. One of them, though, sent me an invitation. They stated they had made some programmatic changes in recent years, and they wanted me to tour their facilities and give feedback. I accepted.

Leadership was eager to tell me about their work. My article had circulated amongst the staff and elicited some lively discussion. Though I was honest with them about some lingering concerns, the tour made it clear that the organization had made some positive changes. Most notably, the mission had chosen to make their nightly chapel service optional rather than mandatory. Testing a hypothesis, I asked how the change had impacted attendance.

My hunch proved correct: More than half of the mission's guests continued to attend chapel multiple times a week. Without being obligated, a majority of mission guests *seek out* spiritual enrichment. The executive director and I connected over a shared observation in our years in this work that unhoused people are often deeply religious long before they ever step foot in our programs.

While we must recognize that people who experience homelessness have rich spiritual lives, it's also the case that this spirituality is often underserved and under-nurtured. Many churches lack the desire or the capacity to welcome them into their spaces fully, and government and secular nonprofits don't incorporate spirituality much either. Faith-based organizations therefore have a unique ability to meet emergent physical needs as well as attend to spirituality in a way that government and other nonprofits simply can't or won't.

But given the ways spirituality is too often weaponized in this space, many faith-based organizations are reluctant to engage in direct spiritual work as part of their services. In this chapter, we will explore three examples of organizations that brave this rocky terrain to great effect, incorporating spiritual and even distinctly Christian practices without manipulating or coercing.

Susan Dunlap, who authored *Shelter Theology* based on her experiences leading a trauma-informed Bible study at Urban Ministries Durham, articulates this poignantly: "Our efforts to tend to the souls of people living without housing does not necessarily mean introducing something new. . . . It usually means nurturing the spiritual resources that people already hold."[1] These exemplary programs demonstrate that thoughtfully nurturing spirituality among the unhoused invites the Spirit of God to transform everyone involved as well as surrounding communities.

* * *

DJ Vincent, founding pastor and CEO of Church at the Park in Salem, Oregon, would like to set the record straight about how faith and homelessness nonprofits can intertwine. "There's a tragic myth," he told me, "that if people actually act and behave in the way of Jesus, that it wouldn't be welcome or accepted. People build a mythology around why they can't partner with different groups or faith communities that is not based in practical reality." I suggested to him that perhaps many who perpetuate these myths do so because they want to choose whom they serve and show respect to—rescue missions often refuse to take government funding not because they are barred from it outright, but because it comes with expectations to serve in ways they disagree with. He shrugged and responded that the only barrier, then, is one that the Christian ministries are themselves choosing to build.

But Church at the Park has chosen a different way, one that so many others could also choose. "When people are judging, they can't connect. If they can't connect, they can't communicate about hope and resources. And if you can't communicate, you can't transform the challenge or people's lives." This is the framework DJ learned from a course on poverty awareness from Portland State University while pastoring a new church plant. After interviewing twenty unhoused people at Cascade Gateway Park while volunteering for the annual homelessness point-in-time count, he recognized a need to understand the issue better as a pastor and alongside his congregation.

After training and preparing, the church began intentional ministry to the Cascade Gateway encampment in 2007. Inspired by Jesus' words in Luke 14 that "when you give a banquet, invite the poor, the crippled, the lame, and the blind . . . you will be blessed," they began a monthly church potluck at the park and invited the unhoused community to eat with them. There were opportunities for prayer, sometimes music, and sometimes discussion of a biblical text, but none were compulsory. Some folks took their food and walked away, others sat down for conversation and ignored the religious elements, and some participated in all of it.

Their stated goal wasn't conversion or even "service," but relationship. As companionship formed organically, the church members simply sought to do "the next best thing" with people. Sometimes this involved coordinating rides, accompanying to appointments, and other one-off helping efforts. Still, the goal was not to fix their homelessness necessarily, but to be in community, together. In that first year, they developed partnerships with other churches to bring meals more frequently, before deputizing a group from within their own church to formalize Church at the Park as its own worshiping community separate from the church that birthed it.

Their approach was in many ways intuitively human: mutual, agenda-less relationship over a shared meal. But for DJ and those who began the ministry, it was also informed by disciplined study of psychology, sociology, and theology. One of the core sources of inspiration was Street Psalms, a religious order grown out of Christian liberation and peacemaking initiatives in urban Philadelphia. Street Psalms preaches a "theology from below," where they "are learning how to read Scripture not 'to,' not 'for,' but 'with' those at the margins."[2]

With this framework, DJ believed that Christian spirituality and theology had something to offer the residents living at Cascade Gateway Park.

> Those frameworks were so ripe for sharing with an unsheltered community who finds themselves below, who find themselves victims of systems of sacrifice rather than systems of mercy. It has been compelling to those who desire a faith orientation that doesn't need to break the agency of other human beings to get them to conform to the behaviors that they want. Instead, they're trying to call people out of systems of violence and into nonviolence and peacemaking.

Inherent in the model of both Street Psalms and Church at the Park is a commitment to partnership. When their work garnered recognition and secured additional resources, they were intentional about maintaining that commitment. The city granted them full use of a community center next to the park, which enabled them to move the meal inside when weather required, as well as to develop a clothing closet and distribute food boxes; park residents not only initiated the clothing and food boxes, but they volunteered alongside the church members to facilitate them week to week. When DJ recognized the need to open the building as a warming center during the colder months, several park residents volunteered to help operate it, and some of them took temporary paid positions to assist further. Many went on to get peer-level certifications and join Church at the Park's growing staff.

This growth was never a primary goal of Church at the Park, but close relationships keyed the outcome. "When you believe the people closest to the problem are actually the ones closest to the solutions, and you're asking them constantly, 'What should we do together?', you just find yourself in the mess of it," DJ explains. Getting messy meant leveraging their growing influence with churches and governing bodies to fund more resources, including shelter spaces, outreach teams, and safe parking.

This gradual growth reached a crisis point during the COVID-19 pandemic. Through 2020 and early 2021, the encampment at Cascade Gateway Park grew rapidly from around thirty individuals to close to three hundred. This was a nationwide phenomenon—while homelessness did not increase during this time, its visibility did. As housed Americans sheltered in place, unhoused Americans banded together to take care of one another and share resources, especially in large parks where they could not go unnoticed. Church at the Park ramped up their work on behalf of and alongside those at the park, even with the limitations imposed by necessary protective measures.

That was, of course, until the city decided that the park needed to be reopened to "the public." Unlike other cities across the country who dispersed these COVID-era encampments by force, Salem decided to open their Oregon State Fairgrounds to the encampments—and asked Church at the Park to run it. In less than a month, they hired forty staff and opened up the fairgrounds for camping. The site ran for several months, but DJ and his staff knew that at some point, they would be asked to close it. Anticipating this, they wrote a proposal to the city of Salem to open and operate eight micro-shelter communities across the region. As of early 2025, they operate three, and they are in the process of opening two more.

At every site, in addition to the services team, Church at the Park staffs a chaplain/pastor—but not to preach or evangelize. This person may provide prayer or other spiritual care to those who ask for it—and many do—but their role is much more communal. They work with volunteers and staff to uphold community values and ethics. They facilitate the weekly "community circles," which invite all residents and staff together to share progress and developments, to air grievances, and to develop opportunities and solutions together.

No matter how much they grow, Church at the Park is committed to the radical simplicity of their relationship model. Whether housed or unhoused, people thrive when they are valued and empowered within a supportive community. "We believe people are the most powerful agents in their own story," DJ professes. "And yet we also believe in the power of the therapeutic community."

When Church at the Park sets "a banquet of love and acceptance for those who need it most," as their tagline states, everyone who sits at the table leaves nourished, both physically and spiritually.

* * *

Anna Taylor McCants can't tell the origin story of FedUp Ministries without telling her own testimony. They are too deeply intertwined—and they are both about people who yearn for something holy and authentic outside of what "traditional church" will accommodate.

Growing up in East Tennessee, her religious life was heavily influenced by the Southern Baptist church, even as she passed through a few denominations in childhood. After her dad passed away while she was in high school, her family clung to the church for community and solace. Her first job, at the age of fourteen, was at a Chick-fil-A. She met a young Christian man and married him, dropping out of college just before she became pregnant. Things were not as picture-perfect as she had hoped, though—her young family often experienced food insecurity, relying on her own parents and eventually food stamps to fill their fridge.

As her life seemed to be conforming to the Southern Baptist ideal, where women are meant to be wives and homemakers, she felt her spirit resisting it. She returned to school, committed to graduating even when she became pregnant a second time—she literally submitted her last final while in labor, giving birth to her son just five hours later. After graduating, an unexpected feeling began to emerge in her: she felt called to ministry, despite her entire upbringing suggesting that was impossible.

As she explored different Christian denominations in search of ones that might affirm a woman's ministerial call, she connected with Luther's theology of service—that Christians are freed not just for their own sake, but to be of service to their community. Anna began the ordination process even before she enrolled in United Lutheran Seminary in

Philadelphia. She and her husband filed for divorce, and she moved herself and her kids twelve hours away from everyone she knew to pursue her not yet fully defined sense of calling. In Philadelphia she met Monique, who became her wife. Because ordination in the Evangelical Lutheran Church of America requires fulfilling an internship call, she, along with her children and Monique, then moved to Michigan for an opening. Then six weeks later, the world shut down for the pandemic.

As a pastor discerning her calling, Anna looked to her new community in Washtenaw County. Access to food, she noticed, was a growing issue. In response to the pandemic, bus routes had been cut, and three low income, predominantly Black neighborhoods were most affected. With no walkable grocery stores, the bus route cuts meant it now took residents forty-five minutes to walk one-way to the nearest one. In response, one neighborhood leader set up a food pantry in her front yard. As Anna recalls, "God showed me communities can take care of themselves. And as 'church' we need to uplift these things that communities are already doing." In Anna's imagination, the work befitting a pastor would be a church-sponsored effort to meet these needs.

Anna heard of another local pastor who had tried and failed to get a food truck ministry off the ground. Combining their visions, they approached the bishop, who agreed to fund it—to an extent. They only granted Anna fifteen paid hours a week to start the new ministry, which she easily exceeded—starting up a nonprofit is a full-time job at minimum. She raised the money for the food truck in six weeks, garnering excitement from the congregations in their synod. In the first year, they served four thousand meals.

Anna asked Tajalli, the woman who had created the food pantry in her front yard, to serve as board president for the new enterprise, dubbed FedUp Ministries—the perfect name for their work. *FedUp* signals their commitment to ensure their neighbors have full bellies, but also that they are fueled by righteous anger at a world that would leave so many neighbors hungry.

Neither Anna nor FedUp were shy about the church affiliation of the initiative, and this aspect was largely well received by those they served. Many would seek out Anna to ask for prayer and encouragement. Even still, Anna wanted to offer more traditional spiritual care and a place to worship for those she met through FedUp. Now ordained, she was serving eleven hours per week as an outreach pastor at King of Kings Lutheran Church in Ann Arbor on top of her work with FedUp. She hoped that one day she'd be able to integrate all of it—the food-based justice work and liturgical church ministry—under FedUp.

This desire began to actualize as the ministry's focus shifted more and more to their unhoused neighbors. As schools, businesses, and bus routes reopened, food access increased for many, leading FedUp to focus their efforts on encampments. As a result, they received a surprising request in the summer of 2021. Two members of the Ann Arbor Police Department approached FedUp, requesting that they bring food to an encampment in their jurisdiction on a weekly basis. The encampment had been the target of frequent 911 calls, yet the police were atypically open to real solutions instead of punishment. It was proposed that FedUp would provide food to accompany other resources (outreach teams, mental health and substance-use support providers, and more).

Anna agreed, on one condition: Ann Arbor police would not check for warrants or arrest anyone while FedUp was present, or else they would not return.

FedUp's regular presence at the encampment led to relationships and connection and, over time, fewer 911 calls. People were getting housed, finding employment, and moving forward with their lives. Anna muses, "If you just are present with people and provide a way for them to receive resources, sometimes that is all they need to move on." When the weather turned cold and most of the encampment's residents moved into a local shelter, FedUp focused their efforts there. They even parked the truck outside the housing complexes where the formerly unhoused most frequently found permanent residence.

In working directly with unhoused people, accompanying them from place to place, relationships flourished and Anna's desire to foster spirituality in the form of a church service only grew. Familiar with coercive and paternalistic models, Anna wanted to be especially thoughtful in her approach. Not wanting to surprise or confuse their regulars by dropping a church service on top of one of their regular weekly meals, she added a new meal on Sunday mornings to exist alongside the new worship service, and she made clear the intention. Even with the goal of the new meal and worship being connected, all are welcome to come and eat without participating in the service, and many do.

The worship service is attended on average by thirty to forty unhoused guests, with a dynamic and open approach to its liturgy. Based on the outspoken opinions of attendees, the church has experimented with styles: whether to include a sermon or more of an open discussion, how much music to feature and what kind, and so much more. The service, called LiftUp, is intentionally steered by Anna—no stranger herself to feeling excluded in worship settings—to "create something with people that allows them to interact with something holy and bigger than themselves, and share what's on their heart."

A spirit of creativity and collaboration governs the space. Much of the decor of the worship space was hand-crafted by the unhoused congregants themselves, from the materials available: metal, wood, even styrofoam. Communion is similarly celebrated with an eye toward practicality. When bread is unavailable, muffins, veggie straws, or whatever is on hand subs in for the body of Christ and gets dipped into the juice. The services differ from week to week, incorporating some structure but leaving space for sharing and expression and all the unexpected directions that a gathering can take. There's room for complexity, chaos, and individuality.

This service is a haven and community for those who experience homelessness and want a church that feels safe for them. Even those who may be sleeping overnight at a church participating in a rotating shelter model will choose to come to LiftUp rather than attend the Sunday service at the church where they're staying. At LiftUp, they are met with warmth and welcome, and their homelessness isn't unusual or something to be feared or maligned. They are safe and free to offer their fullness of self to God and one another.

Anna, through her own journey of faith, is uniquely equipped to hold this space. In all the ways her calling and identity burst out of the confines her upbringing imposed upon her, she now creates spaces to experience and participate in the sacred for those who have experienced a different, though familiar, rejection from religious participation. While literally feeding neighborhoods across Southeast Michigan, she spiritually nourishes herself and a host of others who find with one another and with God a place to belong—unabashed and brazen as themselves. The Lutheran synod now fully supports her call here, extending her full-time to serve FedUp Ministries since 2024—an affirmation of her identity, hope, and spiritual journey all at once.

* * *

Deacon Dave Larrabee, the pastoral director for The Lamb Center in Fairfax, VA, has had to fire a few Bible study leaders—and he'll do it again if he has to.

"We're very careful about screening," he insists. He looks for leaders who are cognizant of the trauma of homelessness and aren't likely to cause more harm. Some Bible study leaders have insisted on preaching a message of condemnation, or on the legitimacy of one denomination to the exclusion of others, and so were asked not to return. There's no glee in this for him; only a clear-eyed commitment to protecting the welcoming atmosphere they've long cultivated.

The Lamb Center has operated for more than thirty years as a daytime drop-in resource center for those experiencing homelessness. They began as a ministry out of Truro Anglican Church, operating in a rented space above a pawn shop with the slogan, "Strong coffee and mighty prayers." In addition to caffeination and intercession, they would offer showers, laundry, and other basic services when possible.

From the very beginning, Bible study was a core offering—always optional, but still central. Dave remembers these studies from when he came to The Lamb Center the first time—not as a staff member, nor even as an unhoused guest, but as someone who'd been court-ordered to complete one hundred hours of community service. He had no interest in the Bible study, and was so prone to skipping it to "check the laundry" that the guests teased him with the nickname Laundry King. Once he'd completed his hours, he left. That is, until he felt compelled to come back. He began volunteering once a week, then was asked to come on part-time, then full-time—even stepping in as director for a stint. Now, he runs the Bible study.

This daily gathering was the subject of a *New York Times* article by Jason DeParle, "At Bible Study for the Homeless, a Search for Meaning." Noting the ways that traditional models lead to coercion, DeParle praises The Lamb's Center's approach:

> The center's Bible study is wholly voluntary and prized by those who join. Whatever benefits it lends the dispossessed, it also offers a reminder that people lumped together as "the homeless" are not an undifferentiated mass but individuals with inner lives and needs that go beyond survival to the search for meaning.[3]

The Lamb Center's understanding of the need for the spiritual extends beyond the Bible study. It is Dave's belief that one of the most Christian things they do is celebrate with those who celebrate and mourn with those who mourn. One of the center's walls holds the nearly two hundred names of Lamb Center guests who have passed away, and Dave keeps a dedicated time on Thursdays for memorial services. Joy is more common, though, as guests celebrate progress in obtaining housing, recovery, or even just commemorating a birthday—another year survived is nothing to sneeze at. It's not uncommon to hear "Happy Birthday" sung overzealously several times throughout the day, even if just for one person. Dave recalled a guest moved to tears by this—he had never had his birthday celebrated before.

Over the course of its thirty years, The Lamb Center has grown in its services, staff, and space. Long gone are the days above the pawn shop. With contributions from more than fifty church supporters across a wide spectrum of beliefs, they designed, built, and opened their ten thousand square foot dream drop-in center—with zero debt.

To ensure real solutions for the guests who pass through, housing case managers, workforce development specialists, nurse practitioners, and dentists all help guests deal with urgent needs as well as long-term goals. Executive director Tara Ruszkowski acknowledges that urgency is what drives The Lamb Center toward best practices, even while faith undergirds it all. "Christ is our North Star," she professes, "but we would say that our best practices are guided by strategy . . . I think the two are harmonious."

The next big project for The Lamb Center embodies their commitment to best practices: fifty-four units of permanent supportive housing to be called Beacon Landing, which broke ground in 2025. While many partners are involved, The Lamb Center's ability to step in financially, with the backing of their supporting congregations, was crucial in getting the funding across the finish line. Church members also showed up to city council meetings in droves to testify on behalf of the project and combat resistance. Like DJ Vincent of Church at the Park, Tara is unconvinced by those who would say faith-based organizations and government can't work together, claiming that Beacon Landing is proof positive that this type of partnership is crucial for "making difficult things possible."

With their stubborn commitment to both spiritual practices and evidence-based ones, The Lamb Center enables a lot of difficult things to be possible—not least of which is being a service provider with the support of congregations across a diverse spectrum of beliefs. These congregations follow their lead, whether by leading a Bible study free of judgment and full of grace or showing up at a city hall to counter NIMBYism. The Spirit moves through The Lamb Center, empowering the organization to lead the congregations of their city despite their doctrinal differences; united by the work before them to serve *all* the needs of the vulnerable among them.

* * *

Speaking to Dave Larrabee, I couldn't stop thinking about Sarah. What she endured at the Grants Pass Gospel Rescue Mission was horrifying in so many regards, but it was the Bible studies that were most traumatizing. I wondered what it might have meant to her if someone like Dave had been screening leaders, keeping an eye out for the types of messages that would be used to harm her and others like her.

In our exploration of churches and organizations thus far, there are some mainline denominations that occur more frequently. Toxic theology, though, has never confined itself to one particular denomination, even as some doctrines correlate to harmful views and thus harmful practices. Because of this, there is no one tradition that has spearheaded the work of ending homelessness. Rather, a wide variety of churches have meaningfully impacted their communities.

Whatever tradition a program stems from, there is a strong connection between program design and the theology that undergirds. *How* spirituality is incorporated becomes a dead giveaway for the content of the spirituality being offered. Groups who mandate attendance are more likely to preach a theology that shames and harms. Harmful theology flourishes where people have no choice but to ingest it.

This dynamic has a parallel in nonreligious service provision. In that world, people experiencing homelessness who turn down available resources are often labeled as "service resistant." Rarely are the reasons for the refusal ever interrogated—the individual may have a dozen reasonable explanations for why the resources are not useful or desirable to them, but their opinion is seldom solicited, let alone actually considered. Instead, politicians, journalists, and even service providers will conclude that something is wrong with the individual, rather than wondering what's wrong with their services. This results in policies that criminalize homelessness, forcing people to accept undesirable and unhelpful services or face jail time.

The same happens with our theology. Church at the Park, FedUp, and The Lamb Center don't have to force attendance because what they offer meets the spiritual needs and desires of those who come. The same can be said of the rescue mission I toured, who demonstrated as much by maintaining strong chapel participation even after it became optional.

If you have to force people to hear your gospel, perhaps the problem isn't with the people, but with your gospel. Your good news can't be that good if those accustomed to bad news can't find something in the gospel worth holding on to. If it isn't a balm to the Sarahs of the world, then your gospel is not worth offering.

Go and do likewise

Susan Dunlap describes her prayer service at the shelter in Durham as "a platform for speaking and enacting a world of comfort and grace in the midst of the horror . . . there is a witness to the persistence of grace, to a light that cannot be extinguished."[4] She could just as easily be describing Church at the Park, FedUp, and The Lamb Center.

The apparent similarities between these three providers speak volumes about the confluence of spirituality and concrete service. Some are obvious: each operates without coercion or manipulation; basic needs are met without religious expectation; conversion is not a primary (or even secondary) goal. But the spirituality in these spaces is more than an *absence* of harmful theology. They offer something that people want and keep coming back for; something that they are not simply asked (or forced) to consume, but that they are invited to participate in, bringing their own sacred contributions to the community.

It's noteworthy, too, that none of these three set out to be large operations. All three began modestly, and FedUp Ministries began even without the intention of focusing on homelessness specifically. In each case, growth came about as the result of deepening relationships. Rather than imposing an organizational vision, they took their cues by listening to the articulated needs of the community. Small, faithful steps led to wholesale transformation, not only on either side of the permeable line between giver and receiver, but in the community at large.

And as these organizations listened closely, they all found themselves gravitating toward housing. As FedUp's truck follows its formerly unhoused patrons into their new dwellings,

Church at the Park and The Lamb Center—on opposite coasts—are making sizeable investments in permanent supportive housing. While so many Christian organizations remain laser focused on models designed to sort out those who are deserving of services from those who are not, those who hold a mutual spirituality are committed to the endgame—a safe and stable home for everyone, where body and spirit can together find healing and worth.

Spirituality in homelessness spaces ultimately comes down to the practice of mutuality. Is spirituality something that the privileged bring to the downtrodden, or is the Spirit alive within all of us, calling us to learn from one another? When we look at people experiencing homelessness, do we see someone who *needs* Jesus, or do we just *see* Jesus? How we answer will go a long way to determine whether the spirituality we foster will harm or heal—and whether it's worth being incorporated at all.

NINE

A Rescued Mission

City Rescue Mission—Oklahoma City, OK

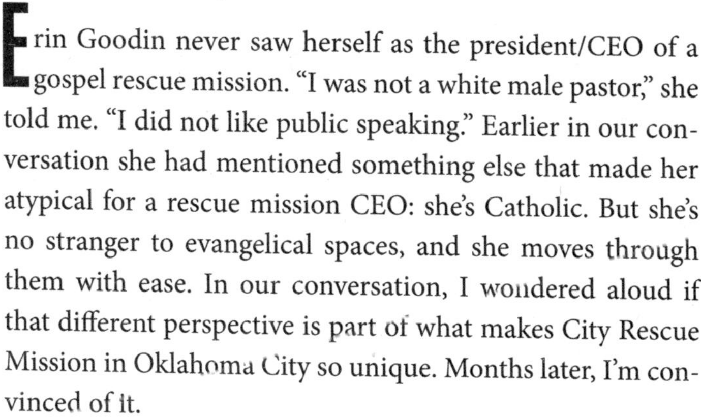

Erin Goodin never saw herself as the president/CEO of a gospel rescue mission. "I was not a white male pastor," she told me. "I did not like public speaking." Earlier in our conversation she had mentioned something else that made her atypical for a rescue mission CEO: she's Catholic. But she's no stranger to evangelical spaces, and she moves through them with ease. In our conversation, I wondered aloud if that different perspective is part of what makes City Rescue Mission in Oklahoma City so unique. Months later, I'm convinced of it.

I've often wondered if gospel rescue missions can be rescued; whether these institutions are too deeply entrenched in harmful modes of thought and practice to ever meaningfully change. There were points in this book's development where I thought that the mission might need to vanish altogether.

City Rescue Mission seemed determined to prove me wrong.

My suspicion comes from experience. Some rescue missions have made seemingly positive changes in their programs that turned out to be more of the same old story. As we explored in chapter 2, there has been a recent effort to change some of the language around practices without addressing the core values. I have met with rescue missions who made even more significant changes, but still harbored ingrained beliefs that their residents were inherently flawed and needed to be fixed rather than empowered. This was apparent in the language used to discuss participants, and even in how they identified stories that could be considered a "success."

So how much greater is my joy to find that City Rescue Mission is for real. Not only does it provide tangible and effective resources in a city I love, but it can also serve as a beacon for other rescue missions, illuminating a path through hard-fought transformation and into a possible future for an institution that so often clings to its past.

* * *

"Amid below freezing temperatures, the state's largest homeless center said they are upholding their standard of choosing which people to take in and which ones to turn away."[1]

So begins a damning piece about the City Rescue Mission (CRM) from KFOR Oklahoma News 4 in January 2018, the same year that CEO Tom Jones would suddenly end his eleven-year tenure. "My hands are tied," he said, referring to his perceived obligation to kick out any shelter residents who couldn't comply with the recovery program's requirements. On the day the article was published, the temperature in Oklahoma City hovered between 10 and 20 degrees Fahrenheit.[2]

At this time, City Rescue Mission's intake procedure that determined who could access their more than six hundred beds began with a urinalysis. If any drugs were detected in your system, even marijuana, you would only be offered a bed on condition of enrollment in the highly intensive and restrictive recovery program. If, after passing the drug test and having been assigned to a bed, you left the mission for any reason and wished to return, you would now only be eligible for the recovery program. If you were a family as opposed to a single individual, you would only be eligible for—you guessed it—the recovery program. "A lot of people were placed into the recovery program who just did not need it. . . . It really stripped them of a lot of freedom," said Makayla Tanquary, who came to CRM as an intern in 2015 and began working in the recovery program in 2017. "In order to get a bed, to get clothed, to have a place to stay, you had to participate in all these things that you probably didn't agree with. It's what you would do to stay inside."

Makayla wasn't exaggerating. The recovery program at that time was a twelve-month commitment, during which participants were not allowed to move into housing or even have a job. They worked instead at the mission, unpaid. Relationships were disallowed outside of legal and "biblical" marriage—if someone was in a relationship when they joined, they were required to break up. Participants were on-site 24/7 with minimal allowances for leaving. Their hours were spent in Work Therapy placements—on-campus job assignments—and participating in daily programming, the majority of which was Bible study. In reality, it was less of a recovery program and more of a Christian discipleship boot-camp—but one that would, for example, kick you out for having too many pairs of shoes or peppermints in your locker. Makayla recalled one woman whose final offense before being exited from the mission was leaving a Bible out on her bed—a violation of the iron-clad bed-making protocol.

For Makayla, the harm of the recovery program was in its combining of a severe curriculum alongside unskilled implementation. When participants weren't being required to memorize and regurgitate entire pages of Scripture, they were guided through the curriculum of Neil T. Anderson, whose books *Freedom from Addiction* and *Freedom in Christ* teach that addiction is fundamentally the result of demonic forces, the only solution for which is conversion and the "freedom" found in Jesus. In Makayla's words, "The whole idea behind the book is that once you're a Christian, you're a new creation. And so anything you struggled with before, you just don't need to struggle with anymore. . . . It didn't get into any coping skills or any type of relapse prevention planning; no real tools to deal with any type of addictive behaviors or trying to maintain sobriety."

Making a moral inventory, a common step in recovery programs, was especially cumbersome and humiliating in this curriculum. Participants had to list and describe every sin they'd ever committed; everything from murder to premarital sex to using a "Magic 8" ball. In a group setting, participants were asked to recount these, many of which were connected to deep traumas, all supervised by staff untrained to handle these types of situations. Makayla noted that most of the leaders of these groups were church leaders who happened to be friends of CEO Tom Jones.

Further underlining the program's all-encompassing religiosity, participants were required to attend a local church every Sunday. While they were told they could attend a Christian church of their choosing, the permitted time allotments to leave the mission limited them to churches whose services fell within the timeframe and were close enough to get to and from quickly. This heavily favored the churches whose theology the mission preferred, some of which would provide rides to and from the mission.

Kayla Thompson, who began at CRM as a bright-eyed and optimistic intern, first started to feel something was wrong at the mission's fundraising galas. The mission held its annual fundraising gala at the National Cowboy and Western Heritage Museum, and it was a lavish affair. Extravagantly wealthy donors, politicians, and local celebrities would sit together for dinner and a program. Kayla knew that some of the mission's residents would be there as part of the program, but she was shocked when she and the residents were made to wait in a back room for hours. "The parallel was uncanny. Some of the most important people of the city, from the world's standards, sat at those tables just behind the door where we were," she said. "But those who had truly lived and been affected by the City Rescue Mission sat behind the doors in a small room, awaiting the signal to come out, wave, and head right back in."

The residents didn't get to speak live—their testimonials were prerecorded and edited down. The video played while the resident stood on the stage, and then they were sent back to the waiting room. "The Gala was all about making those with big checkbooks feel good about the difference they were making, in the pretty room, with the fancy dinner, far away from the Rescue Mission or its residents," Kayla said. When she started her own nonprofit in her hometown in Maine, she made sure to do things differently, operating the Love Alliance as a fundamentally relational, person-centered organization.

* * *

So how does a mission uproot these entrenched, backwards, harmful practices and transform into a housing-first, trauma-informed service provider beloved by its community? The conclusion from everyone I spoke with was unanimous: it all came down to the shy, Catholic accountant who took over the Mission in 2017.

Nearly everyone I interviewed for this book could be considered an idealist. I spent a lot of time talking with people who are earnest and passionate about what they do and how they do it. While Erin Goodin clearly has ideals and passion and leads from her heart, she was also refreshingly direct and focused on data and outcomes; not in the sense of achieving numbers for their own sake, but out of a belief that outcomes reflect the quality of the program.

Perhaps this was the foundational shift. Where previously the most celebrated outcome was a religious conversion, regardless of whether the participant remained dependent on the mission's curriculum and structure, Erin hoped to see people leave the mission and step right into housing and stability. Early in her tenure, the data just didn't reflect that. Instead, people were leaving the program early and often, whether due to expulsion for rules violations (including some of the outrageous examples described earlier) or choosing to return to the streets rather than contort themselves to fit the mission's rigid mold. Erin knew that changes needed to be made if people were going to stay long enough to benefit from the mission's resources. Her first step was to allow for people who had been exited from the mission a pathway to returning. She described her change in methodology as a desire to "keep people in instead of looking for ways to keep people out." In this spirit, she did away with the urinalysis in her first month as CEO and overhauled the rules and expectations placed on participants.

Equally on Erin's mind was how to account for those who didn't leave within their first few months, and in fact never seemed to be able to leave at all. Few were really taking the next step, at least not in the way she hoped to see. Folks were "graduating" from the recovery program in that they were completing the curriculum, but rarely were they achieving independence, stability, or any material outcome. Under Erin's leadership, the staff became laser-focused on housing, making it the core goal and conversation piece for case managers. When I spoke to her in May of 2024, she reported that in the last nine months they had housed 108 families, 254 kids, and 118 single adults.

What surprised me most about the story of City Rescue Mission was the community's reception to the changes. Unlike the experience of Monroe Free in Knoxville (as relayed in chapter 2), City Rescue Mission's donors were not just open to change—they were demanding it. The KFOR story of the mission turning away people in the cold had added to a growing sense that the mission's extremism was making homelessness worse, not better. Poised with data and the support of the community, Erin and City Rescue Mission have made a monumental transformation that the donors and community are able to fully embrace.

It doesn't hurt that faith and spirituality are still a core component of the Mission, now voluntary. Chapel services are held every day, but no one is required to attend. The recovery program, formerly the program into which so many were unnecessarily funneled, is now entirely optional. Those interested in the recovery program are informed up front of its Christian bent and more formal structure, and many choose it specifically for that reason, with no coercion or promise of special benefits over those who don't choose that program.[3] In fact, Erin noted that while both programs are housing-focused, those in the recovery program usually take longer to get housed because they want to work the program first.

Despite the name, this is in line with Housing First principles—the model is about removing prerequisites for eligibility and access, not mandating in what order an individual should resolve their homelessness. If a person chooses to seek something like treatment or financial stability before living independently, honoring that decision is a crucial component of the Housing First emphasis on choice and agency.

* * *

Under Erin's leadership, Makayla was free to transform the recovery program into one she was proud to lead—one that focused on trauma-informed care and professional services. The days of outdated, misguided devotionals led by ill-equipped church members came to an end and were replaced with thoughtful, evidence-based curriculum: anger management, emotional wellness, relapse-prevention. The program was scaled back from a year to six to eight months, and the burdensome requirements were dramatically curtailed. "Work Therapy" changed from grunt work around the mission to partnerships with local businesses to learn trades, which could provide an on-ramp to employment. Bible study groups transitioned to peer support groups, led by actual specialists trained in facilitation and best practices for recovery. Relapses are now met with compassion and care rather than derision and exclusion.

Because the recovery track is entirely optional and is billed from the outset as a faith-based program, they do maintain the expectation of weekly worship-service attendance. However, a new flexibility and agency is baked in. No longer are there imposed time restrictions that limit which churches can be attended. Recovery clients are encouraged to attend the community that best aligns with their values and needs—even if it falls outside of the Christian tradition. *Community* is the essential component. If a Muslim client wants to attend Jumu'ah Mubārak (Friday prayers) at their mosque, this meets the requirement. Despite the many changes to the recovery program, City Rescue Mission has kept this around to prioritize communal life outside of the mission, believing that whenever a resident's stay is complete, it will be their community that catches them.

This emphasis on community extends beyond the local faith community. City Rescue Mission agreed to play an essential role in the city's recent Key to Home Partnership, an initiative to secure direct housing placements for people living in encampments. Erin and her team, whose work had largely been focused on shelter and daytime programming for participants, would now undertake direct encampment outreach and landlord engagement. In our conversation, Erin stated matter-of-factly, "We want what's best for our community, and working together, we can do a whole lot more than staying siloed and by ourselves."

The Key to Home partnership has been an enormous success that signals not just what's possible for gospel rescue missions, but for cities. Since September of 2023, fifty organizations have signed on to play a role in the effort, which set some audacious goals—one of them being to reduce chronic homelessness by permanently housing five hundred individuals before the end of 2025. In the first year, they far surpassed the midway point, housing 332. City Rescue Mission's role in helping secure the units through soliciting and negotiating with landlords has been a crucial and celebrated aspect of the effort's success.[4]

And the galas? Suffice to say, format and content were given a serious overhaul. There was one story that Erin was particularly eager to share. Five years ago, a young shelter resident had all her hopes for housing and a future hanging on a potential college scholarship. While in this limbo, she read about the mission's annual luncheon and bought a ticket to attend. Just before the luncheon, she got the news that she'd been awarded the scholarship. She hasn't missed the annual luncheon since—last year, she sponsored a whole table.

The pride City Rescue Mission takes in its graduates bleeds into their hiring. Rather than hiring based on people's faith commitments and earnest intentions, the mission hires for competencies and experience. In particular, they prioritize *lived* experience of homelessness, especially if that experience includes having lived at the Mission. Sixty-five percent of the Mission's current staff have lived expertise of homelessness, and Erin is convinced that is a key part of their transformation.

> I believe in our clients. I believe in the people we're serving, and they then in turn want to work here and want to give back and help other people and walk with them. That's why we're successful. They are the hands and feet of Christ. They are our mission.

Told you she was an idealist.

Go and do likewise

The story of City Rescue Mission fills me with a lot of hope. Perhaps they can serve as a blueprint for other missions to follow in bringing the *real* mission back to the forefront. Though City Rescue Mission's initial shortcomings and subsequent choices may not apply to every context, many practical ideas and themes are replicable anywhere.

First and foremost, there is no substitute for a willingness to learn and change. This is what all the great individuals and organizations throughout this book continue to demonstrate: a posture of humility and collaboration that allows trends, data, best practices, and the voices of those harmed by existing practices to challenge who they are without becoming defensive. If rescue missions could adopt this posture—one I consider deeply Christian—then they would quickly become dedicated to the things City Rescue Mission holds dear: relationships, dignity, and truly *ending* homelessness.

It's also evident that leadership has to hold these values for there to be any significant transformation. Throughout my research and my own experience, it's proven true again and again that an organization takes on the strengths, flaws, and ultimately the character of its leadership. In many cases this is the CEO or executive director, the leadership team, or sometimes the board. Regardless of who it is, if leadership shifts, so goes the organization.

But no leadership is forever, and change doesn't always last. What makes the story of Monroe Free in Knoxville different from the story of Erin Goodin in Oklahoma City? In Oklahoma City, the community demanded the change, and embraced it when it came. For the leader hoping to guide transformation amidst a suspicious public, this might feel like an impossible task. This, then, becomes a call for the rest of us to do the hard work of narrative change, collective action, and advocacy that not only makes it possible for a rescue mission to change, but is prepared to insist upon it.

Erin probably would have made these changes regardless. But if donors, the local news, and the general public hadn't been so energized about the mission's need to do better, her tenure might have been short-lived. She may have found herself working as a mere interim before another, more "traditional" leader could step in.

Our role as community members—especially Christian ones—is to hold our institutions accountable to the *mission*. Simply claiming Christ should not be enough to earn our support. We must ask hard questions about expertise, values, practices, and outcomes. We must insist that institutions see Christ *in* those they serve, regardless of whether his name happens to be on their tongues. And if they can't meet these basic standards, then we must take our support elsewhere. Gospel rescue missions do not hold a monopoly on the church's calling to the poor. The mission endures . . . with or without the rescue mission.

Conclusion

On a visit to San Diego, I was invited to dinner with a small group of concerned and activated Christians who wanted to pick my brain. We talked about all the initiatives necessary to turn the tide of homelessness and, over the course of an hour, the conversation turned more and more bleak. An air of defeat thickened around us as we considered the work it would require, how vast and all-encompassing it would be, and how much would yet be outside our control.

We got to discussing how often decisions relating to crucial initiatives like affordable housing are made in unexciting local gatherings such as zoning commissions or city council meetings. I mentioned how important it is for supporters to show up to these in order to counter NIMBYs, who often show up in full force to little opposition. A curious resolve came across the face of the pastor who had invited me to the dinner. "Okay, so you're saying I have to start going to all of our local council meetings. All right, when do they meet? Can someone look it up? . . ." Even as his words suggested a renewed commitment, his body and face betrayed the mounting stress. I thought he might burst—we all might have.

In that moment I remembered a piece of wisdom I had learned from people much braver than me and more seasoned in organizing toward systemic change, and I interrupted him. "Hang on—*YOU* don't have to start going to all the meetings, on top of everything you're already doing. *WE* have to start doing it." And suddenly, the anxiety we had lost ourselves in was punctured. We drew breath, our shoulders lowered, our voices calmed. And we began discussing all the ways that the needed work could be shared. His role as a pastor and steward of their church's land certainly called him to significant work, but that others—perhaps retired folks, students, or stay-at-home parents—could attend virtual city council meetings to speak up for the unhoused and to let others know when it would be time to show up in greater numbers. Some could write op-eds, and still others could conduct direct outreach and mutual aid, each according to their skills, capacity, and passion. Suddenly, it felt like the capacity to take meaningful action was again in our grasp.

Throughout these pages, we've seen a wide and yet non-exhaustive breadth of templates for this work. The stories display individuals and organizations successfully addressing this multifaceted crisis, whether by focusing on a single facet or several. Yet none of them can solve the crisis alone, not even in their own cities and neighborhoods. In reading their stories, I urge you not to see a checklist, but rather a menu—a diversity of approaches that may be applicable and replicable in your unique situation. We are not each called to do everything, but merely to do our part.

The harvest is plentiful, yes, and the workers few—but we're far from alone. To turn the tide, we need a strong coalition of people with vastly different resources, gifts, and life experiences. To every person who has ever asked, "What can *I* do about homelessness?," the first step must be to turn *I* into *We*. Little can be accomplished with a single actor—or even many single, detached actors—trying to accomplish a gargantuan task. But when *we* organize, nothing is impossible.

This is not to say there won't be a cost. As the previous stories show time and again, and as remiss as I have often been to say it, I do hope that *we* can include rescue missions too.

* * *

Early in the development of this book, I was far more flippant about the future of rescue missions. A friend set me straight, reminding me that missions represent tens of thousands of desperately needed shelter beds across North America. This is not to excuse how rescue missions have governed this resource, but to acknowledge that it may be well worth our time and effort to win them over. Doing so requires a nuanced view of the role shelters ought to play in our communities—my own feelings about which changed when I moved from California to Minnesota.

In my time in Los Angeles, shelters had become part of a political effort to justify criminalization. Under the 9th Circuit court ruling in *Martin v. Boise* and Los Angeles municipal codes, authorities were restricted on the extent to which they could conduct sweeps and ticketing of unhoused people until enough shelter beds were provided in a particular area.

After a decade-plus of not investing in shelters, suddenly city council was greenlighting shelters right and left. Having been party to some of these efforts only to later see the underlying intent play out to the detriment of our unhoused neighbors, my suspicion was well-founded. In a world that has successfully ended homelessness, we will need very few shelter beds that triage emergency housing loss into robust, permanent offerings.

But we're not there yet, and thus our continuum of care needs shelters. Families with children, seniors, women fleeing abuse, and LGBTQIA+ people especially need quality, dignifying shelters that protect them from the elements and other dangers to which sleeping in a tent makes one vulnerable. Now that I live in Minnesota, where low temperatures can cause irreparable injury and death within minutes if unsheltered, I see how my view was an overcorrection to what I'd witnessed in LA. Shelters are a crucial part of what we offer to people who experience homelessness for short-term safety while awaiting permanent solutions.

That said, we cannot lose our focus on these permanent solutions. Having a robust shelter infrastructure without affordable permanent housing simply shifts the bottleneck indoors. Shelters, while providing a needed lifeline, can (intentionally or not) hide homelessness from the general public without resolving it. In Los Angeles, an effort to rebrand "shelter" to decrease stigma led to the opening of "Bridge Housing" sites. Intended to be temporary, these giant tent structures were erected and filled with those unhoused in the immediate vicinity. Residents, who remained stuck in the system with few to no housing options, began referring to them as "Bridge to Nowhere."

And so rescue missions—and the tens of thousands of shelter beds they represent—are a crucial resource we can't afford to lose at a moment where permanent solutions feel far off. It's all the more important, then, that they be part of a larger continuum, rather than "bridges to nowhere" or, worse, screening grounds for who is worthy of housing and who isn't. This requires the transformation of values that we've already established, but it also requires a willingness to participate with the broader nonprofit sector and governments.

Heartened by City Rescue Mission's work in Oklahoma City, I wondered if CityGate Ministries might be undergoing any larger scale transformation. After all, John Ashmen had stepped away as their leader after sixteen years, handing the reins to Tom DeVries, a tenured executive in international missions and leadership development. In early 2025, they overhauled their website, removing much of Ashmen's content, including the "8 S Words." An updated "Mission, Vision, and Values" page still includes language of "life transformation," but it appears alongside "ending homelessness" and "best practices." Perhaps the change in leadership would be accompanied by broader changes?

I decided to attend their annual conference, that year held in Phoenix, Arizona. About a month before the conference, with my travel arrangements already solidified, my registration was suddenly canceled and my fee refunded. After a few weeks without communication, I received an email from Tom, explaining that he had made the decision to bar my attendance.

Due in part to my critical *Sojourners* article from years earlier, and the lack of communication afterward, Tom doubted my intentions. Despite my clarifying my aims, the decision stood. But despite not being able to attend, CityGate made the recorded sessions available to the public for purchase. I listened to all of the keynotes and plenary sessions, and a sampling of the more than a dozen breakouts, to find some indication on which direction CityGate might be heading.

Some sessions truly surprised me. In one plenary session, Tom DeVries took the stage to encourage the attendees that humility necessitated a willingness to learn from *anyone*, before introducing three researchers from Harvard on the topic of religion and public health. Only one of the researchers was a Christian, and while all three promoted the idea of spirituality as a core component to healing, one of them spoke extensively on the value of religious pluralism. The session extolled missions for incorporating spirituality into their work, but not to the exclusion of non-Christian forms.

Dozens of breakout sessions ran the gamut: from fundraising to board development, programming, handling growth, and so much more. An individual from Light of Life Rescue Mission in Pittsburgh shared about viewing diversity, equity, and inclusion from a biblical perspective. In an "Ask Us Anything" session, seasoned leaders fielded hot-button questions like how to place transgender clients in gendered shelters. (There was no clear consensus among the speakers or attendees.) One of the sessions, led by someone of Nashville Rescue Mission, focused on how attachment theory can give insight into how mission guests relate to themselves, one another, staff, and even God. He challenged those present to consider how trauma influences behavior, and even lamented how often his lens as a mental health professional isn't shared by other staff and reflected in policies.

Many of the stories he shared, however, reflected a calloused and demeaning approach to his clients—especially women. He repeated a conversation he claimed to have frequently with female clients who are bragging about their new, amazing romantic partners, and shared his common response: "He's got problems and I don't even have to meet him. . . . Because he's in a relationship with you."

A few weeks after the conference, Tom DeVries expressed interest in connecting over the phone. Our forty-minute conversation was friendly and wide-ranging. I summarized my concerns with gospel rescue missions and CityGate, especially under his predecessor. He engaged with all my issues and questions, even if I found some of his responses more satisfying than others. Overall, I still don't know quite what to make of Tom DeVries, and I suspect he likes it that way. He struck me as a leader who likes to walk comfortably among both conservatives and progressives and seek compromise. In the grand scheme of the history of CityGate, perhaps this is a positive development.

While I want to celebrate all the small ways that rescue missions are experiencing or spearheading positive changes, I suspect a wholesale identity shift is needed—or, at the very least, an identity clarification. Are they fundamentally a Christian evangelism ministry, or are they a shelter who does what they do because of Jesus' inspiration? It's okay for some shelters to be decidedly Christian in their approach, curriculum, and structure—some unhoused people may choose to live in that setting. Even shelters with high barriers and expectations may be desirable if someone freely *chooses* it—the same way someone might freely submit themselves to a personal training program in order to achieve a goal of running a marathon.

At present, though, the role religion plays in these spaces is often unclear, and people enter them due to the dearth of would-be alternatives as much as anything else. Transparency regarding the program model, beliefs about what causes and resolves homelessness, and what role faith is expected to play in a guest's life would empower volunteers, donors, and especially potential clients to make the choices that fit their needs.

This also means that rescue missions that choose to focus on people who desire their particular methods must have the humility to recognize that their solutions aren't for everyone. Rather than simply say that they do things their way, for their reasons, and that it helps certain people, prominent mission leaders have instead prescribed their model as the solution to homelessness and then made efforts to shape funding and policy to match their approach. While I hope that rescue missions will demonstrate the humility to adapt best practices, they could at the very least stand to the side as a faith-based alternative, rather than in the way as an obstacle to good policy.

* * *

My hope for the mission of ending homelessness does not rest on whether or not gospel rescue missions will embrace a transformation. As we have seen, there have always been alternative ways of living out faith for the sake of the poor and unhoused. There are so many reasons to maintain hope—from those documented in this book, to those limited space forced me to omit, to those I still have yet to encounter.

The settlement house movement of Jane Addams and Mary McDowell illustrates that from the gospel mission's inception there were Christians who raised concerns and established alternatives—to love Christ and house people without preconditions—and it changed the world. Without Addams and the Hull House, modern social work would not be what we know it as today. There are still more than nine hundred active settlement houses in the United States.

A kindred spirit of Addams, whose work I could not fit in my historical survey, is Dorothy Day of the Catholic Worker movement. Her founding of Catholic Worker houses, where the poor and houseless lived, communed, ate, and rallied, was, like Addams' efforts, borne out of a deep faith. Through her houses, writings, and protesting, Day catalyzed and inspired movements around labor rights, anti-war sentiment, and poverty and homelessness, to name just a few. Her work continues to inspire and challenge, and there are more than 175 Catholic Worker houses active worldwide today.

There were so many more stories I hoped to tell in this book, but either brevity or an inability to make contact precluded their inclusion. I wanted to tell you about how two church friends in Washington, DC, began doing street outreach, and how that became the National Alliance to End Homelessness, one of the most influential advocacy and education organizations in the country. I hoped to tell you about Mercy Housing, founded by a few Catholic sisters who were disturbed by seeing families being evicted in Omaha, Nebraska, and how the work they started has been responsible for housing fifty thousand people across forty years. I wanted you to hear about Sunrise Community Church in Austin, Texas, and how they went from merely answering the door when a few unhoused people knocked to becoming the largest service provider in the county, developing new technology to aid people in getting out of homelessness and into housing faster.

Two larger organizations, Family Promise and Habitat for Humanity, could each have warranted their own chapters. Both have long histories of serving folks in the midst or on the brink of homelessness, but with very different models specializing in particular populations. How each has evolved in terms of their model and their interfacing with faith communities is fascinating, but alas, for another time.

The stories captured, though, are the greatest source of my hope. Getting to meet in-person or virtually with so many like-minded souls across the country—exchanging inspirational stories and successes, failures, and heartbreaks—was the blessing of a lifetime. As much as they are meant to inspire others to join in their work, I constantly thought of how much hope they might give just to one another. Gospel rescue missions have CityGate to join them, pour into them, and bring them together regularly. The churches and organizations I spoke with don't have any such unifying support system.

And so I hope that this book allows them, and all those who are aligned in work or in spirit, to feel less alone—as it did for me. And in seasons that feel especially hopeless—as homelessness rises and political forces feel more immovable and reckless than ever—we will need each other to persevere.

This book began out of my own hope: that there were stories worth telling about people of faith dedicated to ending homelessness; that there was something going on with gospel rescue missions worth talking about; that there are people out there that don't want to just do *something* about homelessness but believe that it's worth whatever it takes to *get it right*. Along the way, my hope has looked like inspiration, awe, curiosity, rage, and some days just going through the motions. Hope can hold all of this, so long as we keep dreaming of a better world in spite of the present one.

But in the end, it is not my hope that I'm writing for, but yours. Only hope could have brought you all the way through these stories to this moment. What will that hope kindle in you? What new possibilities will emerge just because you dared to dream, found some fellow hopers, and got to work? Is anything impossible with such hope?

If your heart can still be broken seeing a person experiencing homelessness; if a pit still forms in your stomach when you see point-in-time count numbers rise; if the thought of a person being outside in the cold while you lie warm in your bed still haunts you—then you are a person of great hope. Don't let it fade.

Your hope is holy, because it aligns with the very heart of God, who is nearest to those who are suffering.

Your hope is messy, because it holds space for righteous anger, sacred joy, and so much in between.

Your hope is embodied, because you are working it out with your hands and your feet, your sweat and your tears.

Your hope is vindicated, because we know from experience and research that homelessness ends when we do the most compassionate and generous thing.

Your hope is validated, because there are tens of thousands of fellow hopers dreaming the same dreams as you are, and bringing them one step closer to reality.

May your hope burn eternal. May it be joined with the hopes of those who experience homelessness, and those who would join destinies with theirs; may it be joined with mine; and may it light our way home.

ACKNOWLEDGMENTS

I am nothing and nowhere without my community—the people who love me into meaning and purpose.

First and foremost, my love, Naomi Wilson—you have loved me for my heart long before I knew all it was capable of. You saw in me what I didn't yet see in myself. And after I fell in love with the work of ending homelessness, you did too. The different ways we work separately and together on this have changed our family, and hopefully our community. Our children learned to love their "outside neighbors" from you first.

To Chase, who has now edited both of my books before they ever went to the publisher—I am so grateful to be the first beneficiary of your keen eye and intellect. Your willingness to poke holes in my logic, arguments, word choice, and—always—punctuation bring out the best possible version of my thoughts and stories. Of course, it doesn't hurt that you're a brilliant thinker on these matters in your own right, pushing me to think more deeply and simultaneously more broadly. (For other writers out there, Chase is available—contact me!)

To my closest friends, some of whom I've known for decades and others who just make it feel that way—your constant encouragement, check-ins, listening, and excitement carried me along. Robbie, Izzy, Matt, Garron, Brandon, Meghan, Layne, and Aaron—you mean the world to me.

To the team at Herald Press who were excited to work with me again, thank you for making this dream come true a second time. Laura Clemons, you encouraged me at just the right moment when I needed to know this book was worth writing, and then against all odds you got to help me mold it like you did my last book. I'm so lucky and grateful.

To "Sarah" and Jared, who agreed to provide irreplaceable insight based on their own lived experiences of homelessness—none of what I do is worth anything if it doesn't hold up the dignity of those whose shoes I've never truly walked in. It was an honor to professionally recognize you not only as those with experience but expertise, and something to offer all of us in seeing the world more clearly.

To all those who gave of your time to allow me to interview you for this book—thank you first for the work you're doing that is so worth sharing. And thank you for taking time away from that work to share it with me—and then to clarify, remind, and correct me on the details—so that I could share it with the world. I hope you are encouraged reading your own stories through my eyes, as well as the stories of your comrades, some of which you'd probably never heard of. Please don't hesitate to reach out to one another, and use me as necessary to be a bridge between you.

To anyone engaged in this work in ways that honor the inherent worth, goodness, joy, and resilience of those who experience homelessness—thank you, and please keep going. We need you more than ever. May this book be simultaneously a balm and a bolt of lightning, tending your tiredness and catapulting you onward.

To all those who have experienced homelessness, in the past or present—I hope these words honor you and all that you bring to the world. I hope you never believe for a second that your lives are worth any less than others. And I hope you lead us all into the type of homecoming we as a culture need, returning to the foundational belief in human dignity and connectedness.

Finally, to my kids Micah and Jordan—daily you teach me the joy and wonder of what it is to be alive, the ways we are connected before we inherit the lies that pull us apart, and that love is the center of all. Thank you for keeping me honest and full of compassion, and reinvigorating my desire to imagine a better world.

With endless gratitude,
Kevin Nye

NOTES

Introduction

1 De Sousa, Tanya, and Meghan Henry. "The 2024 Annual Homelessness Assessment Report (AHAR) to Congress." HUD USER, 2024. https://www.huduser.gov/portal/sites/default/files/pdf/2024-AHAR-Part-1.pdf.
2 Quayum, Sajidul, Caren Love, and Patrick Hunter. "Everyone Counts 2020–2022—Results from the Third Nationally Coordinated Point-in-Time Counts of Homelessness in Canada." Housing, Infrastructure and Communities Canada, January 26, 2024. https://housing-infrastructure.canada.ca/homelessness-sans-abri/reports-rapports/pit-counts-dp-2020-2022-results-resultats-eng.html#toc_5.1.
3 Arthur Riley, Cole. *This Here Flesh*. New York: Convergent, 2022. 101.

Chapter 1

1 Prime, S. Irenaeus, and A. S. Hatch. *Jerry McAuley: His Life and Work*. Edited by R. M. Offord. New York: The New York Observer, 1885. 26.
2 Trattner, Walter I. *From Poor Law to Welfare State*. Sixth Edition. New York: The Free Press, A Division of Simon and Schuster, 1999. 53.
3 Prime, *Jerry McAuley*, 184.
4 Conwell, Russell. *Acres of Diamonds*. Project Gutenberg Literary Archive Foundation, 1913.
5 Conwell, *Acres of Diamonds*.
6 Carnegie, Andrew. *The Gospel of Wealth and Other Timely Essays*. New York: Century Co., 1901.
7 Prime, *Jerry McAuley*, 178, 179.
8 O'Reilly, John Boyle. "In Bohemia." Boston: The Pilot Publishing Co., 1886. 14–15.
9 Pope-Levison, Priscilla. *Building the Old-Time Religion: Women Evangelists in the Progressive Era*. New York: New York University Press, 2013, 158.
10 Addams, Jane, Robert Archey Woods, and Franklin Henry Giddings. *Philanthropy and Social Progress: Seven Essays*. New York: T. Y. Crowell and Company, 1893.

11 Pope-Levison, *Building the Old Time Religion,* 157.
12 Field, Chris. "Samuel H Hadley—From the Guttermost to God's Uttermost." ChrisFieldBlog.com, August 27, 2008. http://chrisfieldblog.com/2008/08/27/samuel-h-hadley-from-the-guttermost-to-god%E2%80%99s-uttermost.
13 Pope-Levison, *Building the Old Time Religion.* 156.
14 Hill, Joe. "The Preacher and the Slave." Joe Hill SLC, 1910. https://joehillslc.org/joe-hill/joe-hill-songs/the-preacher-and-the-slave/.
15 Reitman, Ben L., and Madeline Kripke. *Sister of the Road: The Autobiography of Box-Car Bertha*. New York: The Macaulay Company, 1937, 50–51.
16 Ferguson, Manie Payne, *T. P. Ferguson: The Love Slave of Jesus Christ and His People and Founder of Peniel Missions*, c. 1900. 31
17 "About Us." LA First Church of the Nazarene, April 30, 2015. https://la1stnaz.org/about-us/.
18 Seath, *Unto the Least of These: A Handbook of Specialized Ministries in the Rescue Mission*. The International Union of Gospel Missions, 1974. 5.
19 Seath, *Unto the Least Handbook*. 6.
20 Seath, *Unto the Least Handbook*. 86.
21 Seath, *Unto the Least Handbook*. 135.
22 Seath, *Unto the Least Handbook*. 145.
23 Seath, *Unto the Least Handbook*. 9.
24 Seath, *Unto the Least Handbook*. 90.
25 Seath, *Unto the Least Handbook*. 84.
26 Seath, *Unto the Least Handbook*. 92–93.
27 Rooney, James F. "Organizational Success through Program Failure: Skid Row Rescue Missions." *Social Forces* 58, no. 3 (March 1980): 911.
28 Rooney, "Organizational Success," 912.
29 Rooney, "Organizational Success," 912.
30 Fagan, Ronald W. "Skid-Row Rescue Missions: A Religious Approach to Alcoholism." *Journal of Religion & Health* 26, no. 2 (June 1987): 159.
31 Backwords, Ace. *Surviving on the Streets: How to Go Down without Going Out*. Port Townsend, WA: Loompanics Unlimited, 2001. 83.

Chapter 2

1 Bouteller, Brian. "February 2025 Newsletter." Gospel Rescue Mission Grants Pass, February 10, 2025. https://gospelrescuemissiongp.org/2025/02/10/february-2025-newsletter/.
2 Ashmen, John. *Invisible Neighbors*. San Clemente, CA: Cross Section, 2009. 93.
3 Ashmen, *Invisible Neighbors*. 96.
4 Lee, Morgan. "Homelessness Is Vexing American Cities. Do Christians Have a Solution?" *Christianity Today*, May 28, 2021.

https://www.christianitytoday.com/podcasts/quick-to-listen/homelessness-cities-poverty-housing-podcast/.

5 Shinn, Marybeth, and Jill Khadduri. *In the Midst of Plenty: Homelessness and What to Do about It*. Hoboken, NJ: Wiley-Blackwell, 2020. 85.

6 Resnikoff, Ned. "America's Homeless Population Is Exploding. But There's a Solution." MSNBC, January 2, 2025. https://www.msnbc.com/opinion/msnbc-opinion/us-homeless-population-record-military-va-rcna185898.

7 Edwards, Dennis R. *Might from the Margins: The Gospel's Power to Turn the Tables on Injustice*. Harrisonburg, VA: Herald Press, 2020.

8 Fagan, Ronald W. "Skid-Row Rescue Missions: A Religious Approach to Alcoholism." *Journal of Religion & Health* 26, no. 2 (June 1987): 169.

9 Fagan, "Skid Row Rescue Missions," 169.

Chapter 3

1 DeYmaz, Mark. *The Coming Revolution in Church Economics: Why Tithes and Offerings are No Longer Enough, and What You Can Do About It*. Ada, MI: Baker Books, 2019. Kindle. loc. 56.

2 This quote comes from an early manuscript of John Cleghorn's book *Building Belonging: The Church's Call to Build Community and House Our Neighbors* (Louisville, KY: Westminster John Knox Press, 2024). The line was omitted from the final version and therefore remains unpublished.

3 Ponder, Kara Young. "How Racism Underpins the U.S.' Homelessness Problem." The Emancipator, December 20, 2024. https://theemancipator.org/2023/11/09/topics/housing/how-racism-underpins-us-homelessness-problem/.

4 Jarrell, Greg. *Our Trespasses: White Churches and the Taking of American Neighborhoods*. Minneapolis, MN: Fortress Press, 2024.

Chapter 4

1 Gallagher, Charles A., and Cameron D. Lippard, eds. *Race and Racism in the United States: An Encyclopedia of the American Mosaic*. Volume 2. Santa Barbara, CA: Greenwood, 2014.

2 Garcia, David, and Eddie Sun. "Mapping the Potential and Identifying the Barriers to Faith-Based Housing Development." Terner Center Berkeley, May 2020. https://ternercenter.berkeley.edu/wp-content/uploads/2020/08/Mapping_the_Potential_and_Identifying_the_Barriers_to_Faith-Based_Housing_Development_May_2020.pdf.

3 Garcia, David, Quinn Underriner, Muhammad Alameldin, and Issi Romem. "The Housing Potential for Land Owned by Faith-Based Organizations and Colleges." Terner Center Berkeley, August 2023. https://ternercenter.berkeley.edu/wp-content/uploads/2023/08/Faith-Based-and-College-Lands-Housing-2023-.pdf.

Chapter 5

1 Wagner, David. "Over 14,000 Vehicles in LA County Are Used as Homes." LAist, July 6, 2023. https://laist.com/news/housing-homelessness/homeless-count-lahsa-2023-rv-car-vans-tents-shelter-vehicles-los-angeles.
2 Emily has created a resource hub for addressing vehicular homelessness that includes guides on starting programs like this, available at VehicleResidency.org.
3 Stivers, Laura A. *Disrupting Homelessness: Alternative Christian Approaches*. Minneapolis, MN: Fortress Press, 2011.

Chapter 6

1 Roberts, Randall. "At Skid Row Karaoke, They Are All Songs of Hope." Los Angeles Times, October 14, 2012. https://www.latimes.com/entertainment/la-xpm-2012-oct-14-la-ca-karaoke-skid-row-20121015-story.html.

Chapter 7

1 Boden, Paul. *House Keys Not Handcuffs: Homeless Organizing, Art and Politics in San Francisco and Beyond*. San Francisco, CA: Freedom Voices, 2015. 21–22.
2 Bonhoeffer, Dietrich, Carsten Nicolaisen, Ernst-Albert Scharffenorth, Isabel Best, David Higgins, and Douglas W. Stott. "Essay: 'The Church and the Jewish Question.'" In *Berlin: 1932–1933: Dietrich Bonhoeffer Works, Volume 12*, edited by Larry L. Rasmussen, 361–70. Augsburg Fortress, 2009.
3 Krinks, Lindsey. *Praying with Our Feet: Pursuing Justice and Healing on the Streets*. Grand Rapids, MI: Brazos Press, a division of Baker Publishing Group, 2021. 72.
4 Krinks, *Praying with Our Feet*, 26.
5 Prime, S. Irenaeus, and A. S. Hatch. *Jerry McAuley: His Life and Work*. Edited by R. M. Offord. New York: The New York Observer, 1885. 59.
6 Lee, Morgan. "Homelessness Is Vexing American Cities. Do Christians Have a Solution?" *Christianity Today*, May 28, 2021. https://www.christianitytoday.com/podcasts/quick-to-listen/homelessness-cities-poverty-housing-podcast/.
7 Gordon, Cam. "Minneapolis Spends $5.5-$7.5 Million Closing Encampments since 2020." Southwest Connector, May 5, 2023. https://www.swconnector.com/stories/minneapolis-spends-55-75-million-closing-encampments-since-2020,35305.
8 Perez, Rudy. "Homeless Encampment Sweeps May Be Draining Your City's Budget." Housing Matters, January 4, 2023. https://housingmatters.urban.org/articles/homeless-encampment-sweeps-may-be-draining-your-citys-budget.

9 DuBois, Nicole, Clare Herbert, and E. Mae Sowards. "Criminalizing Homelessness Worsens the Crisis, Research Shows." National Alliance to End Homelessness, February 4, 2025. https://endhomelessness.org/wp-content/uploads/2025/02/CriminalizingWorsensTheCrisis_NAEH_2-4-25.pdf.
10 Fort, Lindsey. "SF 2880." SF 2880 as introduced - 93rd Legislature (2023–2024), March 13, 2023. https://www.revisor.mn.gov/bills/text.php?number=SF2880&session=ls93&version=latest&session_number=0&session_year=2023.
11 Name changed by request.
12 Lester, Terence. "What Does MLK Jr.. Have to Do with Homelessness?" *From Streets to Scholarship* (blog), January 18, 2025. https://imterencelester.substack.com/p/what-does-mlk-jr-have-to-do-with.
13 Lester, "What Does MLK Jr."

Chapter 8

1 Dunlap, Susan J. *Shelter Theology: The Religious Life of People without Homes* (Minneapolis, MN: Fortress Press, 2021), x.
2 "Our Mission." Street Psalms. Accessed April 3, 2025. https://streetpsalms.org/about/.
3 DeParle, Jason. "At Bible Study for the Homeless, a Search for Meaning." *New York Times*, November 4, 2024. https://www.nytimes.com/2024/11/24/us/bible-study-homeless.html.
4 Dunlap, *Shelter Theology*, 27.

Chapter 9

1 "'My Hands Are Tied,' State's Largest Homeless Center Turns Away Addicts Unwilling to Get Help." KFOR Oklahoma News, January 2, 2018, https://kfor.com/news/my-hands-are-tied-states-largest-homeless-center-turns-away-addicts-unwilling-to-get-help/.
2 "January 2, 2018 Weather History in Oklahoma City Oklahoma, United States," Oklahoma City, January 2, 2018, https://weatherspark.com/h/d/8231/2018/1/2/Historical-Weather-on-Tuesday-January-2-2018-in-Oklahoma-City-Oklahoma-United-States#metar-13-52.
3 At the time of our interview, about 16 percent of the Mission's clients chose the recovery program over the emergency shelter program.
4 Dickerson, Brett. "26 Rehoused off OKC Streets in Key to Home Partnership." *Oklahoma City Free Press*, November 26, 2024. https://freepressokc.com/26-rehoused-off-okc-streets-in-key-to-home-partnership/.

THE AUTHOR

Kevin Nye is a writer, speaker, advocate, and nonprofit director specializing in homelessness and affordable housing. He speaks and writes to both religious and secular audiences. His writing includes *Grace Can Lead Us Home: A Christian Call to End Homelessness*, and he maintains a biweekly newsletter called *Who Is My Neighbor?* Nye lives in Minneapolis with his wife Naomi and their sons Micah and Jordan.